**Building Library
Collections**

Related Lexington Books

Librarians as Professionals
  William Joseph Reeves
Publishers and Libraries: A Study of Scholarly and Research Journals
  Bernard M. Fry and Herbert S. White
Books and Publishers
  Michael Lane with Jeremy Booth
Perspectives on Publishing
  Edited by Philip G. Altbach and Sheila McVey

Building Library Collections

Policies and Practices in Academic Libraries

Hugh F. Cline
Loraine T. Sinnott
Educational Testing Service

LexingtonBooks
D.C. Heath and Company
Lexington, Massachusetts
Toronto

Library of Congress Cataloging in Publication Data

Cline, Hugh F
    Building library collections.

    1. Libraries, University and college—United States—Collection development—Case studies. 2. Collection development (Libraries)—Case studies. I. Sinnott, Loraine T., joint author. II. Title.
Z687.C58   025.2'1877'0973   80-8602
ISBN 0-669-04321-4

Copyright © 1981 by D.C. Heath and Company.

All rights reserved. No part of this publication may be reproduced or transmitted in any form or by any means, electronic or mechanical, including photocopy, recording, or any information storage or retrieval system, without permission in writing from the publisher.

Published simultaneously in Canada

Printed in the United States of America

International Standard Book Number: 0-669-04321-4

Library of Congress Catalog Card Number: 80-8602

To Lynn, Hugh, and Sean

Contents

	List of Figures	ix
	List of Tables	xi
	Preface	xiii
	Acknowledgments	1
Chapter 1	**Academic Libraries: Organization, Structure, and Function**	1
	Major Functions of Academic Libraries	1
	Types of Materials Acquired	5
	Organization of Academic Libraries	8
	Current Developments	11
Chapter 2	**Project Design**	17
	Project Background	17
	Methodology	20
	Data Analyses	29
Chapter 3	**Profiles of Seven Academic Libraries**	33
	Earlham College	34
	Stockton State College	37
	Brown University	41
	The Pennsylvania State University	46
	The University of North Carolina, Chapel Hill	51
	University of Wisconsin, Madison	56
	University of California, Los Angeles	59
	Summary	65
Chapter 4	**Fund Allocation and Expenditures**	69
	Fiscal Environment of Collection Development	70
	Fund Allocation: An Overview	76
	Patterns of Fund Allocation among Seven Academic Libraries	79
	Expenditures by Format and Discipline	80

Chapter 5	**Item Selection**	95
	General Overview	95
	Item-Selection Procedures in Seven Academic Libraries	99
	Item Selection in Six Disciplines	118
	Conclusion	126
Chapter 6	**Organizational Theories and Social Change**	133
	Organizational Theories	133
	Policy Implications	143
	A Concluding Note	159
	References	161
	Index	165
	About the Authors	171

List of Figures

1-1	Typical Organizational Chart for an Academic Library	10
2-1	Sample Interview Schedule	25
3-1	Organizational Chart of Earlham College Library	35
3-2	Organizational Chart of Stockton State College Library	39
3-3	Organizational Chart of Brown University Libraries	43
3-4	Organizational Chart of The Pennsylvania State University Libraries	48
3-5	Organizational Chart of The University of North Carolina, Chapel Hill, Libraries	53
3-6	Organizational Chart of University of Wisconsin, Madison, Libraries	58
3-7	Organizational Chart of University of California, Los Angeles, Libraries	61
4-1	Academic Libraries' Acquisitions and Their Cost	72
4-2	Breakdown of Academic-Library Expenditures	74
4-3	Typical Academic-Library Yearly Acquisitions	75
4-4	Resource Allocation: Principal Decision Makers	77
4-5	Discipline Groupings	82
5-1	Item-Selection Communication Patterns	97
5-2	Fund Allocation	116

List of Tables

3-1	Institutional Summary Data, 1977-1978	66
3-2	Library Summary Data, 1977-1978	67
4-1	Growth in Academic-Library Resources and Expenditures on Materials	71
4-2	Increases in the Prices of U.S. Publications	73
4-3	Distribution of Materials Expenditures by Format and Discipline Categories, Earlham College, 1977-1978	83
4-4	Distribution of Materials Expenditures by Format and Discipline Categories, Stockton State College, 1977-1978	84
4-5	Distribution of Materials Expenditures by Format and Discipline Categories, Brown University, 1977-1978	85
4-6	Distribution of Materials Expenditures by Format and Discipline Categories, The Pennsylvania State University, 1977-1978	87
4-7	Distribution of Materials Expenditures by Format and Discipline Categories, The University of North Carolina, Chapel Hill, 1977-1978	88
4-8	Distribution of Materials Expenditures by Format and Discipline Categories, University of Wisconsin, Madison, 1977-1978	88
4-9	Distribution of Materials Expenditures by Format and Discipline Categories, University of California, Los Angeles, 1976-1977	89
4-10	Serials Commitment for Each Dollar Spent on Monographs	90

Preface

This book is addressed to several audiences. First, we intend to demonstrate to our colleagues in the social sciences that there are a number of interesting characteristics of academic libraries that add important new dimensions to understanding the structure and functioning of organizations. Second, we anticipate that this material will be useful for instructional purposes in upper-division and graduate-level social-science courses as an example of comparative organizational case studies. Third, we expect that it will be used as a text on collection development in graduate library schools. Fourth, we hope to demonstrate to professional librarians the potentially fruitful insights concerning the practices of academic librarianship that emerge from a social-science organizational perspective. We plan to share with them the social-science prism of organization, structure, and function. Finally, the book is intended to be of interest to a wide variety of persons concerned with long-range planning for academic libraries, including library directors, administrators in higher education, and staff members in public and private funding agencies.

This book analyzes collection-development policies and practices in seven academic libraries, drawing on two theoretical perspectives: analyses of the structure and function of complex organizations and analyses of resource allocation. The study used the methods typically employed in anthropological field research. The analyses draw on data collected during ninety-two person-days of fieldwork, including interviews with 340 academic librarians, faculty members, and college and university administrators. The interview data have been complemented by field observations and material collected from statistical summaries and reports.

The project was organized to ensure a dual return on the resources invested. It is intended that this book make a basic contribution to the social-science study of complex organizations. The data collection and analyses have been structured to provide information and perspectives on a number of policy issues currently facing academic libraries. This attempt at a dual payoff reflects the authors' commitments to policy-relevant social-science research.

Chapter 1 discusses libraries from the perspective of the social-science study of complex organizations. After pointing out that libraries have not been included in the major focuses of social-science research on complex organizations, the chapter provides a brief description of the structure and function of academic libraries generally. The chapter also introduces to the reader unfamiliar with library organization some of the common vocabulary. It discusses the major functions of libraries, the types of materials they acquire and make available to users, and current developments in the profession. Chapter 2 presents a brief history of the project itself and a description of the research methodologies employed.

Chapters 3 through 5 are the major data chapters in the book. Chapter 3 presents short profiles of the seven institutions. It includes information on both the host institutions and the academic libraries, to give the reader some sense of the organizational context in which the libraries function as well as the user communities to whom the libraries provide services. Chapter 4 describes how the libraries allocate their resources to obtain materials for the support of instructional and research programs. Chapter 5 describes how particular books, periodicals, and other materials are identified and selected for addition to the libraries' collections. In addition, this chapter discusses the selection procedures for a number of interdisciplinary and cross-disciplinary programs.

Then chapter 6 presents analyses of five theoretical issues in the study of complex organizations: social change, authority structures, professionalism in an organizational context, boundary maintenance, and multiple constituencies and conflicting goals. These topics, traditionally discussed in many organizational studies, are enriched considerably when analyzed in the context of academic libraries. This final chapter also delineates policy implications relevant to future activities of academic libraries in four areas: library instruction, special collections, microforms, and research.

Acknowledgments

This research was supported by grants from the Planning and Assessment Studies Program, National Endowment for the Humanities, the National Enquiry into Scholarly Communication, and Educational Testing Service.

It is impossible to acknowledge the invaluable assistance rendered by all the librarians, faculty, and administrators who so graciously and effectively provided the raw material on which the analyses reported here are based. The appreciation due to the following library directors is also extended to all their colleagues: Charles D. Churchwell, formerly university librarian, Brown University; Russell Shank, university librarian, University of California, Los Angeles; Evan I. Farber, librarian, Earlham College, Richmond, Indiana; James F. Govan, university librarian, The University of North Carolina, Chapel Hill; Stuart Forth, dean of university libraries, The Pennsylvania State University; Raymond A. Frankle, director of library services, Stockton State College, New Jersey; and Joseph H. Treyz, director of libraries, University of Wisconsin, Madison. Our profound appreciation is also extended to Duane E. Webster, director, Office of Management Studies, Association of Research Libraries, for his invaluable aid in all aspects of the project. As senior consultant, Mr. Webster assisted in every phase of the design, execution, and dissemination activities. This book simply would not have been possible without his support. We also wish to acknowledge the intellectual and financial support of Edward E. Booher, director, and Nazir Bhagat, technical director, National Enquiry into Scholarly Communication; and Stanley F. Turesky, assistant director for evaluation and assessment studies, Office of Planning and Policy Assessment, National Endowment for the Humanities.

Helpful comments on an earlier version of the manuscript were received from David Breneman, The Brookings Institution; Richard DeGennaro, director, University of Pennsylvania Libraries; Ernest Frerichs, dean of the graduate school, Brown University; Warren J. Haas, president, Council on Library Resources, Inc.; John McDonald, director of university libraries, University of Connecticut; and David Stamm, Andrew W. Mellon Director of the Research Libraries, New York City Public Library. Additional clarity was obtained with the help of Melanie Isaacson, Catalog Department, Princeton University Library; Donald Koep, director, Princeton University Library; Charles Osborne, collection development officer, Northwestern University Libraries; and Gertrude Sinnott, Geological Survey Library.

Finally, we wish to record our indebtedness to William W. Turnbull, president, Winton Manning, senior vice president, Samuel Messick, vice president, and other officers and staff of Educational Testing Service for providing the facilities and intellectual environment that so fruitfully support this type of research. In particular, the administrative support of Eugene Horkay and Irma Kienitz, the editorial assistance of Elsa Rosenthal and Lois Harris, and the extraordinary efforts of Lois Barrett in preparing the final manuscript are gratefully acknowledged.

1 Academic Libraries: Organization, Structure, and Function

Complex organizations have been defined in many ways by social scientists. Three features are commonly found in the literature to delineate *complex organizations*:

1. A collectivity of individuals who have reached some minimal agreement to cooperate in accomplishing common goals
2. A structural differentiation of tasks and specific labor assignments among collectivity members
3. A shared recognition of the boundaries of the organization as they pertain to both members and nonmembers

This broad definition encompasses libraries as well as labor unions, hospitals, schools, business organizations, prisons, military units, political parties, and numerous other organizations. A number of different, yet complementary, perspectives have been employed in the study of complex organizations, including communication patterns, management theory, interpersonal relations, organizational development, and control structures.[1]

A review of the social-science literature on complex organizations reveals that little research has been completed on academic libraries from the perspective of complex organizations. With few exceptions,[2] students of formal organizations have not focused their attention on libraries. This book intends to expand the social-science literature on complex organizations by adding a class of organizations which presents a number of new perspectives. Furthermore, because academic libraries are currently undergoing many rapid changes, detailed analyses of these organizations may shed new insights and perspectives on social change in formal organizational settings.

Major Functions of Academic Libraries

There are over 3,000 libraries associated with postsecondary-level educational institutions in the United States. These include two-year community colleges, four-year state colleges, and universities with undergraduate degree programs and a full complement of graduate and professional schools. Increasingly, many institutions within this heterogeneous group are expanding their activities in continuing-education and other nontraditional programs. Despite this wide variety of educational activities and clientele, all academic libraries perform a number of common functions. We have found it convenient to divide these functions into six categories. However, it should be pointed out that, as in all complex organizations, these functions overlap substantially in the activities they encompass. Therefore, they are interdependent in individual execution and complementary in overall organizational goal accomplishment. Nevertheless, for purposes of analysis, it is useful to distinguish among the following categories: collection development, acquisitions, cataloging, circulation, reference, and special collections.

Collection development is a term encompassing a variety of activities designed to ensure that a library includes in its holdings the books, periodicals, and other materials required to support the instructional and research programs of the host college or university. Collection-development activities may involve library staff, faculty, students, administrators, and representatives of commercial vendors or jobbers of library materials. Particularly when discussing the selection of books, those involved in collection development usually distinguish between current and retrospective titles. The term *current* refers to books which have been published or otherwise made available in the present or preceding year. *Retrospective* refers to books which have not been so recently published or distributed; therefore these may not be readily available from publishers or distributors. The distinction between current and retrospective also applies to periodicals, but it is much less clear when applied to other materials.

In practice, the procedures used in selecting current titles differ from those used in selecting retrospective materials. Current additions result from monitoring the announcements of new publications and selecting those consistent with the collection goals of the institution. Retrospective additions are typically made to fill gaps in the existing collection. Gaps are most often noted by user demand for missing titles or by checking the collection against standard bibliographies.

We have found it useful to distinguish between fund allocation and item selection in analyzing collection-development activities in academic libraries. *Fund allocation* is the process of deciding what proportion of the budget for materials will be assigned to various library units or expenditure categories, for example, the chemistry branch library, reference department, Slavic bibliographer, replacement of missing books. Funds can be allocated in two ways: by format of materials, that is, books, periodicals, microforms, and so on, or by substantive areas. Substantive areas may be designated by scholarly discipline (sociology, biology, engineering, and so on), geographical area, or historical period.

In practice, allocations are often made according to some combination of format, scholarly discipline, geographical area, and historical period. Libraries vary in the manner in which they accomplish fund allocation. Allocation decisions may be the responsibility of the library director, assistant director, collection-development officer, or a committee of librarians or faculty. Procedures usually reflect perceived needs of the user community, historical patterns, and the preferences of particular librarians.

Item selection is usually a more decentralized decision-making process than fund allocation. The responsibility to expend allocated money is assigned to a number of materials selectors, that is, bibliographers, reference librarians, branch librarians, academic departments, individual faculty members, or committees of faculty. The procedures they follow to spend funds vary considerably. The major influences on item-selection procedures include the size of the allocation, relative emphasis on current *versus* retrospective purchasing, use of special purchasing plans, and involvement of those whom the fund most directly serves. In the process of adapting to these factors, each library appears to have developed its own unique approach.

In addition to fund allocation and item selection, collection development encompasses a number of other activities, including *evaluation*, *location*, *weeding*, and *preservation*. Collection-evaluation activities are designed to assess both the strengths and the gaps in specific subject areas. Evaluation includes efforts to measure the levels of use of various portions of the library's holdings. Circulation data, especially those generated by computer-aided systems, provide some information on the use of materials outside the library; but measuring in-house use is a particularly elusive problem. Location refers to the decision-making processes which determine where holdings will be placed—in the main library, a branch, a special collection, or a remote location for less frequently used materials. Weeding is the process whereby librarians remove obsolete or unused holdings from the collection to be discarded. All records of weeded materials must be removed from the library's files. Finally, preservation refers to those activities designed to identify and repair items whose physical condition has deteriorated to a point which precludes further use. Inspection of materials may occur as they circulate or in periodic inventories of the collection.

All these activities are usually implied by the term *collection development*. Many academic librarians prefer to use the term *collection management* to connote this broader perspective. However, in this book the primary focus is on fund allocation and item selection, reflecting the collection-development priorities of the librarians we interviewed.

Once the decision has been made to add an item to the library's holdings, the process of acquisitions, the second function common to academic libraries, begins. Included in acquisitions are those clerical tasks associated with ordering materials, monitoring deliveries, and approving payments. The terms *collection development* and *acquisitions* are frequently used interchangeably, thus causing some confusion. But collection development usually refers to the intellectual aspects of deciding which materials will be added to the collection, while acquisitions connotes the clerical aspects of orders and deliveries. The process of acquisition usually starts with a preorder search to ensure that the title is not on order or already part of the collection. If it is not, the process continues in the following order:

1. Collection of sufficient bibliographic information describing the item to allow precise specification of the order
2. Identification of the appropriate supplier
3. Preparation and dispatch of an order
4. Monitoring of delivery
5. In case of nondelivery, initiation of a claim
6. Verification that received items match orders
7. Initiation of procedures for payment

Before items are made available to users, they must be cataloged and prepared for circulation. Cataloging, the third common function, records, describes, and indexes the holdings of a library. This information determines the number and kinds of access points for each item, standardizes the access points, and uniquely identifies all materials to preclude duplicates and gaps in the collection. Among other things, the description includes author, title, publisher, publication date, edition, number of pages and illustrations, size of the item, and a classification code or call number for reference and retrieval.

Cataloging is a detailed and complex process governed by an elaborate set of rules. A librarian might easily devote an entire professional career to mastering all the intricacies of developing bibliographic information for the extraordinarily diverse materials received by academic libraries. Computer-supported networks for sharing cataloging data such as the Ohio College Library Center (OCLC), Research Libraries Information Network (RLIN), and Washington Library Network (WLN), are now in existence and have considerably changed the workload of catalogers. Presently, in most libraries bibliographic information about titles is entered on cards, which are then filed in drawers. But in the future more and more academic libraries will store their cataloging records in computer memory, allowing both users and library staff to access information concerning library holdings via on-line computer terminals or computer-generated microform catalogs.

Technical or end processing, including those tasks which prepare a title for shelving and circulation, is usually included in a cataloging department.

Call numbers are placed on the spines of books, and selected bibliographic information is entered within books. Pockets for circulation cards and, if used, special devices for security against theft are also inserted at this point. Jackets or covers may be placed on certain types of books, phonograph records, or audiovisual materials to lessen wear and tear or facilitate shelving.

Once all the cataloging and technical processing tasks are completed, the item is ready for circulation, the fourth function of academic libraries. Circulation systems vary widely, ranging from completely manual systems to fairly complex, automated systems. The latter may automatically produce overdue notices and compilations of statistics on the use of the collection. They may allow the library to determine quickly where a book is and whether a given patron has violated any circulation policies.

The fifth function of academic libraries is reference. Reference services assist users in gaining access to the collections. Reference librarians provide instruction to undergraduates, graduate students, faculty, and often the public in using reference tools to identify materials relevant to their instructional or research activities. More recently, reference librarians have been assisting users in searching bibliographic files stored in computer memory and organized to allow a user to identify and retrieve references and abstracts by substantive classifications.

The last function common to academic libraries involves the development, maintenance, and use of special collections. Special collections entail aspects of all five functions mentioned above. A special collection is a gathering of material for a particular purpose. The material, for example, may be of a special format, on a specific subject, or produced in a particular historical period or geographical area.[3] Using this rather general definition, one might call a reference collection or a collection of federal documents a *special collection*, but more often the term refers to materials which are collected and organized to facilitate advanced research activities on a highly specialized topic such as the history of printing. Thus, special collections are particularly relevant to university libraries and their attendant research programs.

Types of Materials Acquired

Having outlined the major activities of academic libraries, we now turn to a description of the materials which libraries acquire, maintain, and circulate to their user communities. However, before doing so, we should point out that the collection of these materials constitutes a statement of the educational goals and policies of the host institution with respect to both instruction and research. At least one of the following motives might be involved in acquiring any item for the collection:

1. Support of a basic liberal-arts curriculum
2. Support of a specific undergraduate curriculum
3. Support of a graduate or professional training program
4. Support of a continuing education or an extension program
5. Maintenance of a reference collection
6. Maintenance of a research collection, which can range from minimal to comprehensive

An item may also be acquired with several purposes in mind. Alternately, an item may be acquired for one purpose and later maintained for another purpose. For example, the current issue of *The Foundation Directory*, a listing of all private foundations in the United States with assets greater than $1 million, may be initially obtained for the reference collection but subsequently transferred to the history-of-philanthropy collection when a new edition is acquired.

Books are the major type of material housed in libraries. But outside professional library circles, it is not widely recognized that academic libraries acquire other formats of materials, and it is important to understand that a substantial amount of library time and resources are devoted to them. These formats include serials, microforms, audiovisual materials, maps, musical scores, and ephemera.

Serials constitute the second largest category of materials in academic library collections. However, the definition of serials is not uniformly applied in all academic libraries. According to the American National Standards Institute (ANSI), serials are continuous sets of publications consisting of separate parts, which are disseminated recurrently, usually with no fixed date for termination.[4] They may include several different types of publication:

1. *Periodicals*—serials which have the same title but are numbered or dated and issued regularly[5]
2. *Newspapers*—serials which are issued frequently, for example, daily or weekly, and cover current events[6]
3. *Annuals*—serials which are issued once a year, for example, annual reports, almanacs, or conference proceedings[7]
4. *Monographic or publishers' series*—book-format publications issued irregularly and expected to continue indefinitely
5. *Irregular serials*—unbound journal- or magazine-format publications appearing irregularly but expected to continue indefinitely
6. *Sets*—materials published irregularly, usually in bound format, and expected to terminate at some unspecified time

In considering the above definitions, it is obvious that there may be some ambiguity in identifying serials, particularly in distinguishing them from monographs. Adding to the confusion is the fact that academic libraries vary in which of the above types of publications they decide to include in their serials counts. Some libraries include only periodicals; others include all six categories. Still other libraries include, in addition to the publications described above, publications of federal, state, and local governments, as well as private corporations, whether issued as serial publications or not.

Because of ambiguities in the types of material which might be considered serials, it is often difficult to get from a library an accurate and reliable algorithm for determining which of their acquisitions are classified as serials. During the course of an interview with the chief of one of the serials departments in our case studies, we received the following definition: "Serials in this library are anything that I say are serials." This should serve as a warning to the reader that data we report as the serials holdings of a library must be interpreted with a great deal of caution.

The next type of material most often acquired by academic libraries is *microforms*, a general term used to refer to any materials which are photographically reduced in size and distributed usually in the form of negatives. When used, microforms must be projected in an enlarged format. According to Rolland E. Stevens, microforms can save money, decrease the amount of required storage space, and make materials available that would otherwise be impossible to acquire or use.[8]

Generally, there are five types of microform:

1. *Microfilm*—a continuous roll of filmstrip, usually 100 feet long, containing photographically reduced copies of previously printed materials
2. *Microfiche*—a sheet of film negative imprinted with sixty to one hundred pages of printed materials
3. *Ultrafiche*—similar to microfiche in format but typically containing several hundred pages
4. *Micro-opaque*—a photographically reduced negative printed on a card or sheet of paper, usually containing one hundred pages
5. *Aperture card*—a punched card for unit-record processing equipment which has one frame of 35mm microfilm inserted

Many academic libraries are increasing their microform holdings, especially of the first three formats. Typically they are acquiring two types of material. The first are back issues of serial publications. These are frequently made available through agreement with microform suppliers and the original publishers of the serials. Some retrospective serials are no longer available in hard copy, and some current issues of serials are published in microform only. Libraries frequently find it economical to reduce storage costs by converting hard-copy serials holdings to microform.

The second type of microform is sets of frequently expensive or rare publications. These sets vary widely in size and substantive scope. They may range from such broad collections as the major literary works in U.S. civilization to more narrowly prescribed collections, such as microfilm copies of major German newspapers from 1900 to 1939. Microform collections frequently contain large numbers of documents, including copies of materials which in original format would be beyond the means of most academic libraries. Offered for a few thousand dollars, they allow academic libraries to obtain valuable and important works at relatively reasonable cost. Unfortunately, too many of these large microform sets have only skeletal devices for describing their content and the location of specific items. Consequently, because it is so difficult to gain access to the materials, they are used infrequently.

The fourth type of material acquired by many academic libraries is in audiovisual form. This label encompasses such diverse materials as films, filmstrips, videotapes, phonograph records, audiotapes, slide collections, photographs, and the many pieces of equipment necessary to project or play them. Audiovisual materials are more commonly acquired by libraries in four-year colleges than in universities. In universities many faculty feel that audiovisual materials are not appropriate for their instructional and research programs. The important exception is medical schools, which make extensive use of audiovisual materials, particularly for individualized instruction.

Many university libraries, in fact, collect no audiovisual materials, but there may be a separate audiovisual department on campus, not under the direction of the library. These departments typically provide services for only in-class use of audiovisual materials. It should be noted that when libraries maintain audiovisual facilities, the emphasis is usually on individual rather than group use of the materials.

In addition to books, serials, microforms, and AV materials, university libraries collect and make available to their users many other items, including maps, musical scores, play and film scripts, materials clipped from newspapers or magazines, manuscripts, and numerical data files stored on magnetic tape. Although collected to a certain extent by all college and university libraries, these other materials account for only a small percentage of the total acquisitions budget. However, some of these materials, such as numerical data files, in the future may increase in rate of acquisition and thus consume a larger proportion of the materials budget.

Organization of Academic Libraries

Having considered both the major functions performed and the materials acquired by academic libraries, we may turn now to describing how these functions are organized for the collection, maintenance, and utilization of library holdings. Figure 1-1 is a highly simplified organizational chart for a typical academic library. Some important observations may, however, be made from it. For example, academic libraries operate under the auspices of a host institution—a college or university—and are, therefore, ultimately responsible for their overall operation and effectiveness to the institution's administrative officers. Thus, the library director reports to a president, chancellor, provost, or dean.

The broken line from the library director to the faculty committee indicates that a faculty committee is often appointed to oversee certain aspects of the library's performance. This immediately suggests one interesting feature of academic libraries. Regardless of whether the faculty has a supervisory or an advisory relationship to the library director, the administration of most institutions of higher education looks to the faculty for indications of effectiveness in library performance. Thus academic libraries are accountable to two different constituencies, the administration and the faculty, who may have conflicting expectations concerning adequate effectiveness of library performance.

In the figure, administration and personnel indicate the usual activities associated with these functions in organizations. However, in many larger academic libraries, there are additional functions of budgeting, long-range planning, and developing computer systems.

Most academic libraries separate their major functions into two organizational components, technical services and public services. Librarians frequently refer to the "two sides of the house," each usually overseen by an assistant or associate library director. Technical services typically have the following departments: acquisitions, cataloging, and serials, the functions of the first two of these having already been described. The third department usually manages the acquisition, cataloging, and claiming or monitoring of delivery of serials. However, in some libraries, tasks connected with serials may be performed by other departments; for example, serials cataloging may be done in the cataloging department. Serials departments may also prepare materials for binding, and in the case of many larger academic libraries, a separate periodical reading room may be maintained by the department, providing easy access to recent, as yet unbound, periodicals. Occasionally the periodical reading room is a unit in public services.

Public services always accommodate a reference function and frequently include circulation and special collections. In large institutions, branch or departmental libraries are often part of public services. Branch libraries may be located in departments or professional schools.

Many librarians spend their entire careers on one side of the house. It is not rare to find individuals in the cataloging departments of large university

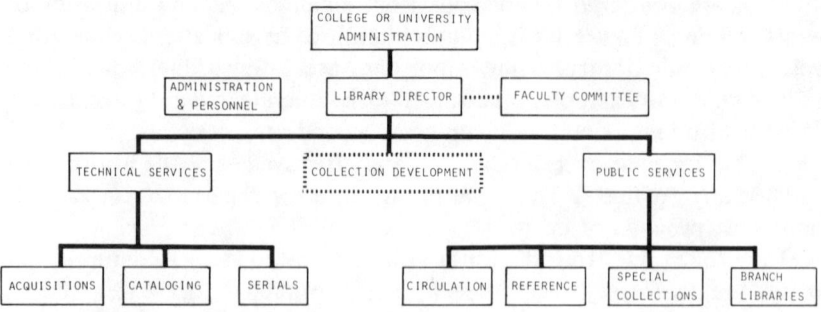

Figure 1-1. Typical Organizational Chart for an Academic Library

libraries who have always been catalogers and who anticipate performing no other task in their professional careers.

Collection development may operate as a department within either technical or public services. It may also operate outside these divisions, reporting to only the library director. In some libraries, primary responsibility for collection development may be assigned to an individual or individuals in units formally associated with other goals. For example, collection-development activities may be assumed by the reference staff on a part-time basis. Or the library director may be primarily responsible for collection development. Thus in many libraries, collection development does not exist as an independent activity. The location and organization of collection-development activities are dependent on the size of a library's collection, the size of the user community, the diversity of the academic program, and traditional patterns of collection-development activities within each library. To indicate the variance in the organizational structure of collection development, we surround the unit in figure 1-1 with broken lines.

In large academic libraries, there is often a collection-development department composed of a large staff of full-time bibliographers. This department is primarily responsible for acquiring material for the system's central library. Bibliographers are expected to keep abreast of current publications; they are also expected to identify needed retrospective materials. There is a division of labor among them in terms of substantive areas, for example, Renaissance studies, international relations, or sub-Saharan African affairs.

Reference librarians are usually those members of the library staff most involved in collection development when it is not an independent unit. Through their interactions with users, these individuals can readily become aware of the instructional and research activities of students and faculty.

Branch librarians are also expected to have this kind of detailed knowledge of student and faculty needs. Indeed, even when an independent collection-development department exists, it is seldom involved with collection development in branches; this is perceived as the territory of the branch librarian.

Current Developments

In this final section of the introductory chapter, we point to a number of current developments within the community of academic libraries relevant to collection development. The order in which these issues are discussed does not imply their importance within libraries. Indeed, the relative importance of a given issue varies considerably across libraries.

A major worry of all academic libraries is their waning power to purchase materials, the problem brought about by the mounting costs of books and periodicals. Using the 1967-1969 period as a base, we find that by 1979 the average price of U.S. hardcover trade technical books increased 160 percent. The average price of U.S. periodicals for the same period increased by 251 percent.[9] Further, the expense of obtaining materials from foreign countries has risen because of the declining value of the U.S. dollar.

This problem could be relieved by equivalent growth in library budgets. But for almost all academic libraries, materials budgets have not been growing at a rate commensurate with inflation. Indeed, for many academic libraries, the 1970s has been a period of stable or declining budgets. With increases in salaries and wages for library employees, as well as in the costs of maintaining and operating the physical plant, the dollars which remain for acquisitions decrease not only in value but also in number. For many libraries the impact of these forces has been a significant deterioration in their acquisitions programs.

Academic libraries are also confronted with the consequences of the pervasive explosion in the production and consumption of knowledge. Expanding populations of information producers and consumers, combined with a growing corpus of knowledge, underlie the explosion. The knowledge base has mushroomed since World War II, and it promises no abatement in the near future. For example, the number of books published per year in the United States has increased from approximately 15,000 in 1960 to over 41,000 in 1978.[10] The emergence of new scientific disciplines has contributed significantly to the knowledge explosion. Specialized fields such as biochemistry, behavior genetics, psychopharmacology, and environmental psychology, which cross several different disciplines, proliferate new monographs, journals, and annual reviews. It is now estimated that over $1 billion is expended annually to maintain almost 500 million volumes in

3,000 college and university libraries, and the number of volumes is increasing at an estimated annual rate of 23 million.[11] The data on the growth of libraries coupled with the impact of declining budgets and rampant inflation make it abundantly clear that libraries are experiencing great financial and managerial problems in both maintaining and expanding their holdings as well as fulfilling their user needs.

In many academic libraries, space problems are becoming particularly acute. The present acquisitions rate is causing some research libraries to double in size approximately every twelve years.[12] Many colleges and universities simply do not have the resources necessary for adding new buildings to store materials. Academic librarians have considered a number of ways to alleviate this situation, including decreasing acquisitions rates, placing less frequently used materials into storage, converting hardcopy holdings to microform, and appropriating reader space in existing physical plants for additional shelving space. But if one wishes to provide the most effective services to users, none of these options seem acceptable.

In some libraries space has become so critical a problem that the shelving of a new holding may require the discarding or remote storage of a title presently in the stacks. Because of tight budgets and limited space, for many libraries the decision to purchase one book may preclude the purchase of another title also appropriate for the collection. These are among the reasons why libraries are leery of purchasing duplicate copies of new titles. For the rarely or occasionally used title, the availability of only a single copy does not interfere with library service. But for an often used title, it becomes highly unlikely that it will be found on the shelf. Thus, although libraries are increasing enormously in actual size, their effective size, as measured by a user's chance of finding the title required, is not keeping pace.

Another serious problem confronting college and university libraries is the deterioration of their holdings. Since the mid-nineteenth century, paper manufacturers have used an alum-resin sizing in their paper which, in the presence of atmospheric moisture, creates sulfuric acid. Books printed on this paper may disintegrate within a thirty-year period. Environmental controls can slow deterioration, but installing the equipment necessary to support these conditions is a costly expenditure which most academic libraries cannot presently afford. Consequently, the stacks of many libraries are littered with the powdered and shredded residues of rapidly deteriorating materials. Research activities are underway at a number of different locations to develop a chemical treatment which would halt further deterioration. Although such a treatment would be a significant breakthrough, it would not reverse present damage. Hence libraries will still be burdened with extensive holdings so brittle that the pages crumble when handled.

Academic librarians clearly recognize that unless a solution to the problem of deteriorating holdings is forthcoming, large portions of their collections will be irreparably damaged and lost. The solution to this problem is not within the grasp of any one academic library, and yet the consequences of not dealing adequately with the preservation problem will drastically affect each library's operation and capacity to serve its user communities.

Another continuing issue for all academic libraries is the requirement of matching library holdings to the instructional and research needs of the host institution's programs. This is not a simple matter of a one-time determination, for college and university instructional and research programs are constantly changing. Student interests and demands for courses change from year to year, new academic programs and research institutes are frequently established, and older ones are terminated. Faculty members' interests change. Faculty retire or move to other institutions and are replaced with new faculty with different teaching and research interests. In order to keep track of this constantly shifting amalgam of substantive interests among the students and faculty, the library staff must continually reach out, make contact with, and become informed about student and faculty activities to ensure that they are in a position to add appropriate materials to the library's collection.

But there is an inherent dilemma in this task for the library staff. In order to remain current or optimally informed in advance about new academic programs, the library staff members must have some level of substantive expertise in the topical area so that they can interact knowledgeably and effectively with faculty members. But how much substantive expertise is necessary for this task? Some librarians feel that it is necessary only to have an interest in a topical area; substantive expertise can gradually be accumulated with experience. There are instances in which a junior library staff member may have responsibility for faculty liaison in a wide variety of departments. For example, one librarian may cover all social and behavioral sciences, including anthropology, economics, political science, psychology, sociology, and statistics. This pattern is not limited to smaller academic libraries. In other instances, a librarian may have graduate training up to and including the Ph.D. in a substantive area and be designated as a bibliographer with collection-development responsibilities in a substantive discipline area, a regional-studies area, or a particular historical period.

The question of appropriate training and expertise for item selectors or bibliographers has prompted much discussion among academic librarians. It may well be, though, that the salience of this issue is declining somewhat as attention has been drawn to the diminishing purchasing power of book budgets. As the number of decisions necessary to buy titles decreases, the justification to maintain a staff of highly trained, and hence costly, personnel for this endeavor dissolves. Indeed, in some of the institutions visited during the preparation of this book, individuals with substantively defined selection responsibilities and matching academic training are losing ground in terms of the prestige they command in the library. Their loss of prestige is very much a function of the decreasing purchasing power of the funds they command.

The reliance in many institutions on blanket orders with commercial vendors is also undermining the need for substantively trained materials selectors. These vendors select materials based on profiles designed by the contracting libraries, arrangements which are particularly efficient and effective when a library is collecting all publications of specific publishers or authors or is collecting comprehensively in a particular field. They also may provide the only economically feasible means of collecting materials in countries with poor documentation about their publications or countries in which limited printings are common. When blanket-order contracts are used, library staff involved in selection may be asked to monitor the performance of vendors. Although substantive expertise may greatly improve this monitoring, whether the cost of the errors avoided compensates for the extra cost of substantive expertise becomes questionable.

A final current development for most academic libraries is the increasing visibility of library operations and the corresponding expectation on the part of college and university administrators of a new level of accountability for these operations. Many academic librarians view this as a most welcome development and consider it both a challenge and an opportunity. Two concurrent developments are promoting the increased visibility of libraries. The first is the production of detailed and sophisticated statistical reports and summaries of many aspects of library operation which emanate from the recently installed computer systems for acquisitions control, shared cataloging, and circulation. These reports tend to be widely distributed both within and without the library, thereby whetting the appetites of many administrators and faculty for further information about library operations. The second development which enhances the new level of accountability is the increased fiscal supervision exercised by college and university administrators over all activities within institutions of higher education. Libraries as well as all other academic units are being more carefully monitored and supervised.

It has been speculated that this increased visibility and closer monitoring of library operations account, at least in part, for the fact that the position of director of an academic library has become an increasingly demanding and difficult role to fill successfully. Several years ago, McAnally and Downs reported that 50 percent of the directors of the seventy-eight largest academic libraries in the nation had retired or resigned within the preceding three-year period. They projected that if this rate of turnover continued, the average tenure of an academic library directorship would be five to six years.[13] Of course, many factors contribute to turnover, but it is certainly true that increased levels of visibility and accountability are significantly changing the nature of the position of director of an academic library.

Notes

1. Probably the best review of the organizational literature can still be found in James G. March, ed., *Handbook of Organizations* (New York: Rand McNally, 1965).
2. See for example, Robert Presthus, "Technological Change and Occupational Response: A Study of Librarians," Final Report to Office of Education, Department of Health, Education, and Welfare, June 1970, Project No. 07-1804; and Elaine F. Sloan, "The Organization of Collection Development in Large University Libraries" (doctoral dissertation, College of Library and Information Services, University of Maryland, 1973). However, several economists have recently studied academic libraries. See Fritz Machlup, *The Production and Distribution of Knowledge in the United States* (Princeton, N.J.: Princeton University Press, 1962); William J. Baumol and Matityahu Marcus, *Economics of Academic Libraries* (Washington: American Council on Education, 1973); and Fritz Machlup and Kenneth Leeson, *Information through the Printed Word*, vol. 3: *Libraries* (New York: Praeger Publishers, 1978).
3. *American National Standards for Library Statistics* (New York: American National Standards Institute, Inc., 1968), (R1974), ANSI Z39.7 p. 19.
4. Ibid., p. 19.
5. Ibid., p. 16.
6. Ibid., p. 16.
7. Ibid., p. 8.
8. Rolland E. Stevens, "Resources in Microform for the Research Library," *Microform Review* 1 (January 1972):9-18.
9. *The Bowker Annual of Library and Book Trade Information* (New York: Bowker, 1980), pp. 456-458.
10. *Statistical Abstract of the United States* (Washington: Government Printing Office, 1979), p. 593.
11. *The Bowker Annual*, 1978, pp. 246-247.
12. Oliver Charles Bunn, W.F. Siebert, and Janice A. Schueneman, *The Past and Likely Future of Fifty-eight Research Libraries, 1951-1980: A Statistical Study of Growth and Change.* (Lafayette, Ind.: University Libraries and Audio-Visual Center, Purdue University, 1966).
13. Arthur M. McAnally and Robert B. Downs, "The Changing Role of Directors of University Libraries," *College and Research Libraries*, March 1973, pp. 103-125. More recently it has been suggested that the average tenure may be somewhat longer now. See Paul Metz, "Administrative Succession in the Academic Library," *College and Research Libraries*, September 1978, pp. 358-364.

2 Project Design

Project Background

The holdings of academic libraries are large and incessantly expanding. The issues described in the last section of chapter 1, such as eroding purchasing power, deteriorating holdings, and an exploding publication market, have created difficulties in just maintaining present levels of efficiency and effectiveness, let alone improving operations. Consequent pressures are causing rapid changes in the structure and functioning of academic libraries. Many features of structure and functioning are more visible when an organization is undergoing change. Thus, for students of complex organizations, it is indeed a strategically opportune time to study libraries. As yet, social scientists have virtually ignored libraries as complex organizations suitable for scientific investigation, despite proliferating studies of many other types of complex organizations and a burgeoning analytic literature.[1]

When we began to explore the possibility of studying academic libraries, we did so with two objectives in mind. The first was to expand the theoretical perspectives of social scientists who study formal organizations. It seemed clear that libraries must possess unique characteristics when compared with other complex organizations. Thus the study of libraries could expand and complement both empirical studies and theoretical writings on organizational structure and functioning. Moreover, we believed that systematic studies of libraries from an organizational perspective might produce new data and insights pertinent to the operation and management of academic libraries.

In December 1977, the staff of the National Enquiry into Scholarly Communication (NESC) encouraged us to submit a proposal to both the NESC and the National Endowment for the Humanities to conduct a study of collection-development policies and practices in academic libraries. The NESC, a large project supported by the National Endowment for the Humanities (NEH), Ford Foundation, Andrew W. Mellon Foundation, and Rockefeller Foundation, was examining all aspects of the creation and dissemination of scholarly knowledge. It viewed scholarly communication as a single system composed of four related units: scholars, professional journals, university presses, and academic libraries.[2]

The NESC coordinated and supported a series of complementary studies to examine each of these nodes in the network of scholarly communication.

It was especially concerned with the humanities and the theoretical, or non-quantitative, social sciences, believing that natural scientists and the quantitatively oriented social scientists had access to more effective systems of information transfer than did the scholars in the humanities. However, we believed that to maintain the broad perspective of academic libraries as complex organizations, it was necessary to include all scholarly disciplines within the scope of the project. This more general approach to studying collection development in academic libraries was acceptable to the NESC and the NEH.

When we first considered studying collection development, we reviewed the four basic research methodologies which can be used to examine complex organizations—questionnaire surveys, simulations, quasi-experiments, and case studies. Although questionnaire surveys have been used in organizational studies with some success, this research design requires that the investigator know the organization intimately. It is always problematic to determine both the salient issues to pursue and the appropriate terminology. In order to design relevant questionnaire items, one must understand the structure and functioning of an organization, as well as its unique practices and vernacular. Usually a great deal of information is required from an organization to complete the questionnaires, and typically a substantial commitment of institutional resources is required. It is unlikely that organizations will participate unless they are offered sufficient incentives, either substantive or financial.

Initially, a questionnaire survey seemed a reasonable approach to a study of collection development, but it did not take long for us to appreciate how complex this process was in academic libraries. Furthermore, the complexity on one campus was not identical to that on another. Terminology varied, as did the complement of individuals involved. Thus to construct pertinent questions interpretable in a consistent manner across a set of libraries would have been most problematic. Identifying the most appropriate respondents for a questionnaire would be difficult without prior familiarity with local collection-development procedures. Such considerations convinced us that a valid study of collection development could not readily be accomplished by survey methodology.

A second methodology available for the study of organizations is simulation. The investigator constructs a set of theoretical statements about organizations from which conclusions can be derived. The derivation is frequently aided by simulating the organization's functioning over hypothetical periods on a computer. Simulations cannot yet be used for systematic analyses of phenomena such as collection development, for they presuppose an enormous amount of detailed knowledge of how organizations function before the model or theory can be constructed. Such general knowledge about collection-development policies and practices simply does not exist.

A third methodology is the quasi-experiment which, in a field setting, attempts to emulate a laboratory experiment, including assignment of subjects by randomized procedures to either experimental or control groups, administration of treatments or stimuli to the experimental group members, and measurements of all subjects both before and after stimuli administration to assess differences.

Under certain conditions, quasi-experimental designs can be very powerful in studying organizations. However, they entail research activities in which a specific treatment or stimulus is applied to the experimental group. In this attempt to study collection-development policies and practices from a resource-allocation perspective, there is no clear-cut stimulus which could be applied to an experimental group of libraries and withheld from a control group.

The data analyses employed in quasi-experiments usually require a substantial number of cases. A minimum of thirty is recommended. It is frequently feasible to use this design when the units of analysis are individuals. However, when organizations are the units of analysis, it is seldom practical to accomplish random assignment and almost impossible to obtain the cooperation of thirty or more organizations.

The fourth design available for the investigation of organizations is the case study. The intensive study of selected units characterizes the case study, which is especially useful for producing insights, stimulating ideas for future research, and identifying major consequences of social change. The utility of the case study is significantly expanded when the design includes several sites which are compared. When several organizations are studied, the investigator uses a comparable set of field methods, including interviews, observations, and the analysis of existing reports and statistical data. Because of the complexity of collection development, a comparative case-study approach offered the most attractive alternative for this investigation.

Case studies are frequently used and often criticized by social scientists. The major problem with the case-study method is its limited generalizability. Since it is an in-depth investigation which requires a substantial commitment of time and resources, a case study is a very expensive undertaking; and comparative case studies are even more expensive. For this reason, investigators usually limit their designs to a small number of units, in this case a small number of academic libraries. Nevertheless, whether the design includes one or several organizations, the generalizability to other organizations is always questionable.

Limited generalizability is not the only problem which confronts organizational case-study designs. Getting organizations to agree to participate in studies which necessarily interfere with day-to-day activities and potentially produce embarrassing results is always a problem. In participating, an organization commits resources, primarily staff time. The allocation of such resources might be considered more favorably if the organization felt that it was getting something out of the exercise. Planning and tact are necessary to gain the cooperation of organizations in a research project, and the investigators should ensure that the organizations receive adequate remuneration of some kind.

Collecting accurate historical data is another common problem in case studies. When examining organizations at one particular time, the investigator must strive to eliminate the biases inherent in retrospective recall. The problems encountered by social scientists in studying past events are well known and documented.[3] Detailed planning for interviews, delineation of objectives of observations, and use of existing documents and reports are all effective methods for verifying the accuracy of historical data.

The use of various methods for collecting data from multiple sources characterizes the case study. The remainder of this chapter is devoted to discussing how these data collection and analysis techniques were employed in this project.

Methodology

Directing our research design was the desire to maximize the comparability of data collected within and across the libraries. This required advance planning of all interviews and observations and adherence to project schedules. Data synthesis and analysis followed predetermined rules for verifying the accuracy of information. Yet compliance with specific guidelines concerning data collection and analysis still leaves the investigator facing the difficult question of precisely what information to collect during the fieldwork. By its very nature, the case study implies comprehensive data collection. However, this is impossible, for the amount of data that can be collected in any organization is infinite. It is necessary to select certain aspects of the organization for emphasis. In this project, the resource-allocation perspective provided the necessary framework.

It was essential that the libraries selected for study be chosen to ensure representative information across the range of collection-development policies and practices. Several criteria were established on which to base selection decisions. First, it was decided that this project should include both college and university libraries, for it was deemed important to compare collection development in institutions oriented primarily to undergraduate instruction with institutions oriented to both instruction and research. Both public and private institutions were to be included since differences in governance and funding procedures might account for differences in collection-development practices. Additional criteria included the size of the existing collection, geographical distribution, extent of faculty involvement in decisions concerning collection development, and salience of collection development as a topic of library priority.

Receptiveness on the part of an organization to participate in a research project understandably varies across institutions. The findings of a project may result in criticism, a reduction of funding, or pressure to modify established patterns of resource allocation. However, the exposure accompanying participation may be viewed as an opportunity. For example, it can provide a forum in which to exhibit an organization's accomplishments. How the prospect of participation is viewed by administrators will depend considerably on their personalities, on problems the organization has recently experienced, and on the willingness of an organization to accept change.

Since participation is a risk for some and an opportunity for others, samples composed of volunteers may be biased. Yet, most often, working with volunteers is the only practical alternative. External or internal forces may push hesitant administrators into participation, but the coercion may produce hostility, which in turn impairs the investigation. Case work in organizations requires the cooperation of management. It is not difficult for alienated administrators to impede the work of a researcher.

To identify sites for investigation, it is useful to consult with individuals having specialized knowledge regarding the organizations. In addition to identifying candidates, these individuals often can facilitate introductions. Consulting with a specialist may result in entering a network of organizations which misrepresents the population of concern to the investigator. This can be avoided by choosing consultants known to have a global perspective. For example, an officer of a national association is likely to be knowledgeable about all members of the association.

In this project, Duane E. Webster, director of the Office of University Library Management Studies, Association of Research Libraries, provided consultation in making selections. Six institutions were initially invited to participate. Unfortunately, one of the libraries declined the invitation on the grounds that it was an inopportune time to conduct such a study. After further consultation with Webster and the staffs of both the NESC and the NEH, the investigators decided to expand the study to include seven institutions, adding two institutions to replace the one declination. The following institutions participated in the study: Earlham College; Stockton State College, New Jersey; Brown University; The Pennsylvania State University; The University of North Carolina, Chapel Hill; University of Wisconsin, Madison; and University of California, Los Angeles.

Much effort was expended in developing rapport with the senior administrators in the seven institutions. Each library director was sent a lengthy letter of introduction and a copy of the project proposal. The letters described the goals of the project, proposed on-site research activities, and provided references which could be employed to assess the investigators' credentials. Subsequent telephone calls were then placed to determine if the library was interested in participating.

We strongly prefer the use of introductory letters, rather than telephone calls, to initiate contacts with organizations. A telephone call not preceded by a letter might prompt a decision before an administrator fully appreciates the implications of the commitment. An administrator, forced into a conversation at an inopportune time, may be unable to provide a thoughtful response. She or he may volunteer the organization but later, after the commitment is more clearly understood, withdraw; or continue participation, but at a minimum level of cooperation. Since a telephone call is a dynamic event, its content cannot be predicted in advance. In contrast, introductory letters allow the investigator more control over the information conveyed in the initial communication. Finally, a letter and its accompanying materials can be readily shared with other staff members; the content of a telephone call is less accurately and conveniently circulated.

Initial visits of one to two days were made to all participating libraries. Agreement to the initial visit required a minimal commitment of organization resources, and there was little reluctance to agree to such a meeting. The visits allowed the library administrative staff to meet us and discuss the project. We also used the initial visits to learn more about the specific characteristics of each library, information which was critical in planning subsequent fieldwork activities. During the visits, interviews were conducted with senior staff members to gather these data. We began each visit with a group meeting with the library director and other key administrative staff. During these sessions of one to two hours, we summarized the project history, theoretical perspective, methodology, and anticipated outcomes. We also answered questions posed by the library staff.

We stressed that we were interested in collecting information to provide objective descriptions of collection-development policies and practices. It was also emphasized that there was no intention of evaluating the performance of any individual library staff member or of complimenting or criticizing any single individual or organization. As outsiders to the library profession, we believed it presumptuous to make such judgments. Any recommendations forthcoming from the project would be directed generally to the profession of academic librarianship. It was also pointed out that no questionnaires would be distributed among the library staff or faculty. This comment was received with universal enthusiasm. Furthermore, only already compiled statistical summaries and prepared reports would be requested.

After the group meeting, individual interviews were conducted with those who had attended the meeting and others identified as good informants on the organization of the library, particularly as it pertained to collection development. These hour-long interviews focused on two topics. First, each person was asked to describe the organization of the unit(s) under his or her direction, including a discussion of task assignments and staffing levels. Second, they were requested to describe fiscal planning, spending, and reporting during a typical budget cycle. Subjects covered included how the total library budget was prepared and how funds were subsequently allocated to various units within the library. An attempt was made to identify the principal decisionmakers in the budget processes.

Planning the fieldwork visits was greatly facilitated by the information gathered during the initial visits. This information helped avoid the scheduling of activities tangential to the project's goals and the oversight of relevant activities. Without such information, it is exceedingly difficult, if not impossible, to identify all appropriate informants for interviews and activities for observation.

Following each visit, we drew up a schedule of interviews, specifically naming each library staff member, faculty member, and college or university administrator we wished to interview. The schedule proposed a day, an hour, and the estimated time required for each interview. Lists of topics to be discussed with each interviewee were also prepared so that the library director could both review the topics and forward the lists to the appropriate interviewees. All materials were sent to the library director with suggested dates for the fieldwork visit. Directors were asked to make a decision based on these materials and their reaction to the initial visits as to whether their institution would continue participating in the study. All agreed to do so.

We recognized that in order to accomplish the tasks of the fieldwork, an advance schedule would be necessary. However, we were also prepared to make adjustments as required. We were aware that we were intruding on a library in the midst of its operations, and staff could not turn their attention solely to our efforts. Hence, the schedule was subject to many exigencies of the institution. During the course of the fieldwork, we were frequently directed to informants or activities which were not part of the original schedule. The schedule had to be adapted to shifting priorities in order to take advantage of emergent opportunities to enrich the investigation. However, it was necessary to exercise considerable discipline to ensure that site-visit objectives were accomplished in the allotted time.

The second, or fieldwork, visits to the libraries varied in length from six to sixteen person-days, depending on the size and complexity of the library. In the initial visits, we conducted mostly joint interviews; but in the fieldwork visits, we usually conducted separate interviews, the exceptions being typically interviews with the library director and, where appropriate, the staff member primarily responsible for collection development.

Fieldwork activities included interviews, observations of routine operations, attendance at staff or special committee meetings, participation in organizational activities, and collection of existing documents produced by the organization. As in most field research, interviews and observations accounted for the largest blocks of time.

Despite valiant efforts to ensure that all members of the library staff were aware of the purposes of the project and the role of the investigators, there was still considerable variation in willingness to talk to the interviewers. Since interviewees cannot be coerced, information gathered in interviews is, for the most part, data submitted by cooperative individuals. The implications for the representativeness of these data have to be considered.

We anticipated that some staff would view us as agents of the library administration—evaluators who had come to assess their performance. Such perceptions might create anxiety and reluctance on the part of interviewees to respond openly. In all the libraries, the administration was supportive of the research effort, and this problem was substantially diminished by the administration's efforts to advise the staff of the project's purposes.

The quality of data collected from an individual during an interview is, in general, a function of how the interviewer is perceived. The project's success depended equally on its procedures and our ability to establish rapport with library staff, the main sources of data. Once the fieldwork was underway, we quickly realized that many of the staff members enjoyed discussing their function in the organization, the activities in which they engaged, and their attitudes concerning various aspects of the library. In general, staff in an organization seldom verbalize their roles, and many appreciate the opportunity to do so with interested and sympathetic outsiders. The novelty of discussing how one spends a considerable portion of one's life is, for many, an enjoyable experience.

As mentioned above, lists of topics to be discussed in each interview were circulated in advance. We hoped that the protocols would stimulate some advance thinking about the topics and establish a context within which to view the interview. We also hoped that information about the interview's content would decrease any anxiety the interviewee might have about the session. Figure 2-1 is a sample of an interview protocol used for a collection-development officer.

The topics pursued in interviews focused on the details of collection-development policies and practices. For example, staff in acquisitions were queried about procedures used to acquire retrospective materials and the details of existing blanket-order or approval plans. These specialized topics were not covered with other interviewees. Yet there was considerable overlap in topics discussed, particularly with the faculty and those library staff members associated with public services. Indeed, for these individuals

INTERVIEW PROTOCOL FOR COLLECTION DEVELOPMENT OFFICER

FISCAL ISSUES

    FUNDING SOURCES
    BUDGET CYCLE AND STABILITY
    RESTRAINTS ANTICIPATED IN A FUTURE OF LIMITED
        FUNDING AND GROWTH IN HIGHER EDUCATION

FUND ALLOCATION PROCEDURES

COLLECTION DEVELOPMENT

    SIGNIFICANT CHANGES IN COLLECTION DEVELOPMENT:
        PAST AND EXPECTED
    ASSESSMENT OF COLLECTION USE AND USER NEEDS
    ASSESSMENT OF COLLECTION STRENGTHS AND GAPS
    IMPACT OF COOPERATIVE ARRANGEMENTS
    STATEMENTS OF COLLECTION DEVELOPMENT POLICY:
        THEIR UTILITY

ITEM SELECTION PROCEDURES

SPECIAL COLLECTIONS

    DESCRIPTION
    FUNDING SOURCES
    USER GROUPS

AUTOMATION

    PRESENT AND ANTICIPATED APPLICATIONS
    FUNDING SOURCES

LIBRARY INSTRUCTION

Figure 2-1. Sample Interview Schedule

protocols appeared very much as in figure 2-1, with some changes made in the subtopics to ensure that the general topics would be meaningful to a given individual. Occasionally general topics were removed entirely because they were inappropriate for a particular interviewee. For example, faculty were not asked about library automation; but this topic did appear on the protocols of almost all librarians and university and college administrators.

The protocols gave structure to the interviews, but by design they also allowed considerable freedom for discussion of additional topics during the sessions. The open-ended statement of topics did not limit conversations, but allowed topics not previously considered to emerge. Although we were sensitive to the problem of "getting off the track," generally, we encouraged interviewees to pursue these points if they were at all relevant to collection development. Indeed, as the fieldwork continued, many of these issues became important subtopics for later interviews.

With such flexibly structured interviews, the flow of conversation actually determines the order in which the topics are introduced. However, it was crucial not to omit topics, for the reliability of our findings depended considerably on interview comparability and confirmation of data across interviews. In many ways, flexibly structured interviews demand greater care by the interviewer than more formal formats. The interviewer must conduct a casual conversation which eventually covers all predetermined topics within a specified time.

In each library, an interview was completed with the supervisors of all major units. Thus, we interviewed the heads of cataloging, acquisitions, serials, microforms, documents, reference, special collections, and branch libraries. In addition to discussing topics previously outlined, unit heads were asked to describe the unit's organization, responsibilities, and staffing level. Also, in each library an attempt was made to interview all staff members who were not unit heads but who were significantly involved in aspects of either fund allocation or item selection.

Faculty from a number of disciplines in each institution were interviewed to determine faculty involvement in collection development. Among these were six common disciplines in all seven institutions: biology, chemistry, English, history, psychology, and sociology. In most instances, faculty were designated official departmental-library liaisons or chairpersons of book committees. In those cases in which no one was formally so designated, the library staff recommended a faculty member who was knowledgeable and could serve as an informant on faculty involvement in collection development.

In each institution an interview was conducted with at least one person in the college or university administration. This was always someone who was concerned with overall fiscal planning and budgeting for the institution and had particular responsibility for determining the budget for the library. Who this administrator was varied from campus to campus but might have been the president or chancellor, provost or assistant provost, dean of the faculty or of the graduate school, or a staff member from the planning and budget office.

Interviews lasted one to two hours. Each interview was prefaced with a description of the project, and all interviewees were given an opportunity to ask questions and clear up any concerns they might have about the project. A total of 340 interviews were conducted during the fieldwork, ranging from 25 to 77 per campus.

We could not predict which interviewees would be cooperative and reliable informants, but some general cautionary measures were taken. Staff on the fringe of organizations are often willing to criticize. It could well be that their perceptions are more accurate than those of individuals more closely tied to the organization. Often senior administrators and others involved in central activities cannot objectively view the strengths and weaknesses of their organization. Thus, fringe members are potentially valuable sources of information, possibly offering information and insights missed by those integrated more completely into the institution. When we spoke to staff perceived as outsiders by their colleagues, we were careful to discern the motives of these fringe members in coming forth with critical remarks. Furthermore, we guarded against being identified as sympathetic with members of the organization perceived by others as deviant or perhaps troublemakers. An investigator's credibility with more established individuals may be jeopardized if she or he becomes identified with individuals perceived as cynics, rabble-rousers, or malcontents. However, because "outsiders" may provide valuable information, they were not ignored. The validity of the information they offered was checked by supplementing it with information from other members of the organization.

Methods for recording the data collected in interviews were specified in advance. A major issue was how to prepare these data to ensure that they could be shared by both authors. Two options were considered. The first was to use portable equipment to make audio recordings of interviews. The second option was to take as complete notes as possible during the interviews and observations and later transform notes to written reports.

The advantages and disadvantages of these options were carefully considered before the investigation began. Recording provides a more complete and accurate rendition of the content of interactions, but it is a costly option. The equipment is expensive to purchase or rent, and transcription of tapes is time consuming. Audio recordings quickly produce a large amount of data, much of which may not be relevant to the purposes of the investigation. The investigator then confronts the task of selecting, from enormous amounts of data, those which are relevant and transforming them into a usable and sharable report. Despite its disadvantages, recording is sometimes essential, especially when a complete record of interactions is necessary. In our opinion, it was not warranted for this project.

The second option, taking field notes, is subject to biases introduced by selection and recall. The researcher rarely is able to write down everything that transpires. For the most part, the researcher notes what he or she perceives as the most important points and may not even succeed at this more limited task. A particularly good interviewee may provide information so rapidly that the researcher cannot fully capture all the important and relevant comments.

No matter what recording method is selected, a researcher must, at some point in the life span of a case study, synthesize the data. If this is done too early, the researcher may incorrectly decide what information is relevant. Crucial perspectives or information may be omitted because the researcher is not yet aware of the salience of a topic. On the other hand, delaying synthesis can result in the accumulation of useless data. The researcher must exercise caution with respect to the timing of data synthesis.

Audio recording captures all interactions within the range of the microphone. Note taking starts the process of synthesizing immediately, and subsequent data reduction and analyses further select and abstract from the original data. Audio recording preserves more of the data for later review; but the collection, storage, and analysis of the enormous quantity of data rapidly escalate project costs. How field data are preserved depends, therefore, on the importance of complete recording of all possible events relative to available resources.

For this project, complete recording was unnecessary. It was decided that notes would be taken during interviews and no tape recording would be employed. Field notes were transformed into narrative written reports as soon as possible after completion of an interview or observation. The narratives comprehensively covered notes taken during the field activities and further elaborated on the points, using information we recalled but did not write down.

As in all case studies, a system for filing data was a crucial aspect of the project design. As the project progressed, we rapidly became inundated with data from the interviews, observations, and documents describing the libraries. The arrangement of these data quickly became a major management problem. Prior to beginning the fieldwork visits, this problem was anticipated, and a system for storing and retrieving the data was ready for implementation. However, a number of modifications were necessary before we obtained an optimal system. In the end, data were organized by different departments within the library and different functions within each unit.

It is the responsibility of each investigator to explain to individuals how the interview data will be used and preserved. All study data were placed in the archives at Educational Testing Service, subject to the rules of access pertaining to this data repository. In practice, this means that no one will have access to the data without the permission of the project director. Scholars with serious interest in using these data for research will be granted access only after obtaining the written permission of the directors of all seven participating academic libraries. Should we no longer be at Educational

Testing Service (ETS), access will be granted by the ETS vice president for research after the same procedures are observed.

We take seriously the responsibility of investigators to protect the right of privacy of individuals. For this reason, only in instances where it is absolutely necessary, in order to make substantive sense of a point, have particular individuals been identified in this book. When individuals are so identified, they are, in all instances, identified by title only.

Data Analyses

Questions of validity and reliability are especially troublesome in case studies. Indeed, they are a problem in any social- and behavioral-science research projects which rely primarily on interviews and participant observation. Anthropologists have had the greatest experience in dealing with these problems in their fieldwork. However, with very few exceptions, the literature in the field of anthropology is not helpful in addressing the questions of the validity and reliability of data. Therefore, it was necessary to devise procedures for ensuring maximal validity and reliability in data collection and analysis.

We focused on obtaining information about activities which add new materials to the libraries' collections. The basic strategy in getting this information for each institution was to ask many individuals the same questions. Each individual took part in some aspect of collection development, and each could give a description of collection development from his or her unique perspective. We recognized clearly that these descriptions would vary, in some cases substantially, depending on a person's position, responsibilities, and range of activities within the library. A central task of our analysis was to review all data collected in both interviews and existing reports to identify the commonalities. The commonalities were taken as the best possible approximation of reality, that is, how collection development is accomplished. The strength of this method relies on interviews with a large number of persons. In practice, no piece of information in this book was accepted as valid unless it could be verified in at least two different interviews or substantiated by library documents.

The book has been given a further structure for comparative purposes by the collection of detailed information on item selection in six disciplines across the seven institutions. Identifying six common disciplines in seven institutions of higher education is not a simple task, since academicians have shown great ingenuity in organizing scholarly disciplines into a wide variety of combinations of departmental structures. Nevertheless, six common areas were identified.

Additional reliability is obtained in the comparative case-study approach. When conducting comparative case studies, the investigator employs similar data-collection procedures to ensure comparability. In essence, the comparative design is a replication of the case study in each of the libraries. There is a common focus on collection development in each institution, and the comparative design ensures uniformity of data collection and analysis procedures.

The question of consistency in the data collected by interviewers is troublesome in studies using case-study methods. We were able to improve the degree of congruence in the notes and transcriptions emanating from interviews. In the initial library visits, most interviews were conducted jointly. Each author kept his or her own notes of the interview, and systematic comparisons were made later. This kind of comparison was repeated at several points. It is possible to report that the agreement between each set of notes and transcribed interviews increased as we progressed. In fact, the notes taken in joint interviews conducted in the last institution were almost identical. Therefore, interviewer reliability is probably fairly high.

A problem that cannot be solved within the context of this book is the question of the relationship of our data to the data which might have been collected, analyzed, and interpreted by two other social scientists. We base our claim that our data-collection methods are reliable on the responses made by the librarians who reviewed the first draft of this book. The reader will have to judge the reliability of the data on the basis of the adequacy of the descriptions of each institution and the logic of the analyses which follow.

All data collected in interviews and existing reports were subsequently reviewed and analyzed with three main purposes in mind. First, the data were synthesized to produce objective descriptions of collection-development policies and practices in the seven academic libraries. Second, the data were reviewed and organized to address a number of theoretical issues relevant to academic libraries as formal organizations. These issues have been discussed at length in studies of other types of organizations, and their formulation and conceptualization can be significantly expanded when libraries as a new class of organizations are appended to this literature. And third, the data were carefully reviewed to identify possible policy-relevant topics concerning the future organization and operation of academic libraries.

Finally, we address the issue of causal analysis in this project and more generally in comparative organizational case studies. To establish causal explanations, three factors are necessary:

1. Covariation
2. Sequence
3. Elimination of all other possible causal explanations

Covariation implies that variable x, the causal or independent variable, and variable y, the effect or dependent variable, always occur or vary together. Sequence implies that the causal variable always precedes the effect or result variable in time order of occurrence.

In most social-science research designs, the first two conditions are not difficult to attain. The problem is the third factor, elimination of all other possible causal variables. Through randomization, one can "control" for other possible causal variables in experiments and simulations. The use of a large number of causal variables in a multivariate analysis provides some control over this problem in surveys using questionnaires. But in case studies, it usually is impossible to eliminate conclusively all other possible causal factors.

Only through the replication of uniform and documented data collection-and-analysis procedures can investigators begin to eliminate other causal factors. In this study, it has not been possible to provide plausible causal analyses. However, causal explanations, where they seem appropriate, are suggested at various points throughout the text.

The need for a set of procedures which ensure more systematic means of data collection and analysis in case studies is patently clear. Until these problems are solved, it is highly questionable that case studies will ever accumulate the data bases necessary for theory building and policy advisement in the social and behavioral sciences.

Notes

1. See, for example, Philip Selznick, *TVA and the Grass Roots* (Berkeley: University of California Press, 1949); Peter M. Blau, *Dynamics of Bureaucracy* (Chicago: University of Chicago Press, 1955); Herbert Kaufman, *The Forest Ranger*. (Baltimore, Md.: The Johns Hopkins Press, 1960); Alvin W. Gouldner, *Patterns of Industrial Bureaucracy* (Glencoe, Ill.: Free Press, 1954); James G. Abegglin, *The Japanese Factory* (Glencoe, Ill.: Free Press, 1958); Gresham M. Sykes, *Society of Captives: A Study of a Maximum Security Prison* (Princeton, N.J.: Princeton University Press, 1958); Rose Giallombardo, *Society of Women: A Study of a Women's Prison* (New York: John Wiley & Sons, 1966); Alfred H. Stanton and Morris S. Schwartz, *The Mental Hospital* (New York: Basic Books, 1954); William Caudill, *The Psychiatric Hospital as a Small Society* (Cambridge, Mass.: Harvard University Press, 1958); Seymour M. Lipset, Martin A. Trow, and James S. Coleman, *Union Democracy* (Glencoe, Ill.: Free Press, 1956); Dov Elizur, *Adapting to Innovation* Jerusalem, Israel: Jerusalem Academic Press, 1970); Chris Argyris, *Organization of a Bank* (New Haven, Conn.: Labor and Management Center, Yale University, 1954); Francis A.J. Ianni, *A Family Business* (New York: Russell Sage Foundation, 1972).

2. The final report of the National Enquiry into Scholarly Communication is published. See *Scholarly Communication: The Report of the National Enquiry* (Baltimore, Md.: The Johns Hopkins Press, 1979).

3. Claire Selltiz, Laurence S. Wrightsman, and Stuart W. Cook, *Research Methods in Social Relations* 3d. ed. (New York: Holt, Rinehart, and Winston, 1976).

3 Profiles of Seven Academic Libraries

In this chapter we describe the participating libraries, their host institutions, and their user communities. Except as noted, the data refer to the 1977-1978 academic year. The profiles provide a context within which to interpret subsequent descriptions of fund allocation and item selection.

With each description of a library, we include an organizational chart. It is, of course, difficult to represent accurately the structure of any organization since not only are changes constantly occurring, but also no chart can reveal the intricate network of interrelationships and interactions that characterize complex organizations. Nevertheless, we illustrate in grossly oversimplified form our approximation of current organizational structures so that we may both summarize library functioning and provide a basis for comparison among the libraries.

Before turning to the profiles, we must digress briefly to alert the reader that although our strategy of studying collection development from an organizational perspective does provide common theoretical perspectives, data-collection methods, and analytic techniques across the institutions, it also produces certain noncomparable elements in the design. After selecting each institution for participation, we identified the chief library officer on each campus and then studied all organizational units which reported to that individual. This procedure provided our working definition of the boundaries of the seven organizations. However, it is frequently the case in universities that not all libraries on a campus report to the university librarian. Law and medical school librarians often operate independently and report to their respective deans. Such independent libraries are not included in this book. Therefore, much of the data presented in the profiles does not include all library activities in each institution; and the data may not agree with the "official statistics" issued by the college or university or other organizations such as the National Center for Educational Statistics or the Association of Research Libraries. All these instances are carefully noted below.

We begin our profiles with the colleges—first Earlham College, then Stockton State College. As expected, the college libraries are smaller and less complex organizationally than the university libraries. Their description should provide a helpful introduction to the university profiles. The university libraries are subsequently presented in the following order: Brown University; The Pennsylvania State University; The University of North

33

Carolina, Chapel Hill; the University of Wisconsin, Madison; and finally, the University of California, Los Angeles. For each institution, we present the distribution of degrees awarded by major discipline groupings. The breakdown of these groupings is provided in figure 4-5.

Earlham College

Earlham College, founded in 1847 by the religious Society of Friends, is a coeducational, residential, liberal-arts college. Presently only about 20 percent of the 1,015 students are Friends. Its 800-acre campus is located on the western edge of Richmond, Indiana, and it includes fifteen academic, administrative, and residential buildings. The ninety-one full-time-equivalent faculty members offer four-year liberal-arts programs in twenty-one traditional and six interdepartmental majors. In 1978 Earlham awarded the bachelor's degree to 199 graduating seniors. The major fields were distributed as follows: sciences, 30 percent; social sciences, 37 percent; humanities, 27 percent; other, 6 percent. Over 60 percent of the graduates eventually enter a postbaccalaureate program. Earlham's endowment is approximately $26 million, and its annual operating budget is $6.8 million. The college is governed by a twenty-three-member board of trustees with representation from the Indiana and the Western Yearly Meetings of the Society of Friends as well as the Earlham College Alumni Association.

The college's library collection, numbering about 240,000 volumes, is housed in two facilities. Lilly Library, constructed in 1962, contains the bulk of the collection, approximately 210,000 volumes primarily in the humanities and social sciences. It also houses the administrative offices; the circulation, reference, and technical-service departments; a special collection of Quaker materials; the college archive; and the audiovisual department with its language laboratory. The second facility, the Ernest A. Wildman Science Library, is located separately in Noyes Hall. Wildman maintains some 27,000 books, periodicals, and government documents in the natural sciences, as well as a substantial map collection.

Figure 3-1 presents the organizational chart for the Earlham College Library. There are seven professional librarians on the staff. The head librarian reports directly to the provost, and all departments report operationally to the head librarian, but audiovisual services has its budget approved independently. At Earlham, technical services are grouped in a single department, and circulation is located in a separate department. Earlham adds between 6,000 and 8,000 books and periodicals to its collection each year, and both its acquisitions and its cataloging can be accomplished by one professional librarian supervisor and a two-person sup-

EARLHAM COLLEGE LIBRARY

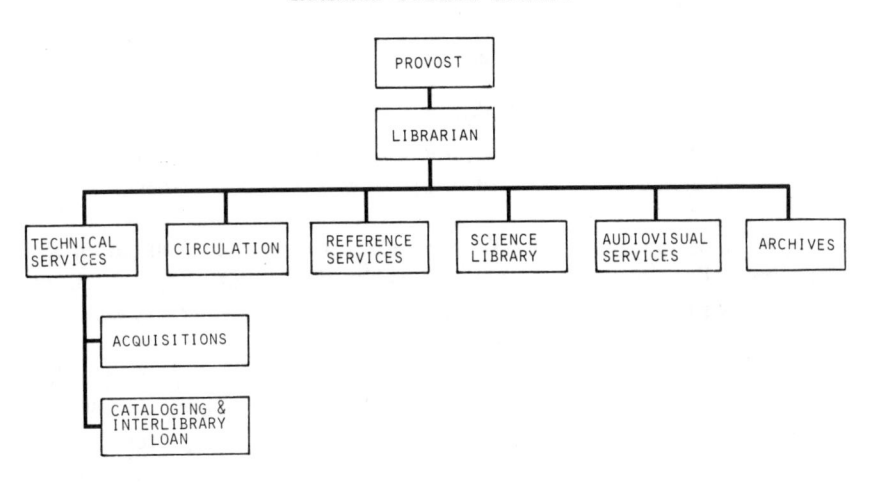

Figure 3-1. Organizational Chart of Earlham College Library

port staff, assisted by part-time student workers. Circulation is also supervised by one professional librarian, aided by student assistants. Although there are only 1.5 full-time librarians assigned formally to reference services, all professionals are actively engaged and strongly committed to reference work in both Lilly and Wildman. Audiovisual services maintains and lends equipment, administers the language laboratory and film rentals, and participates in media production. Audiovisual services is not concerned with the collection of media materials. The library maintains a slide collection of 25,000 and a phonorecord collection of about 1,700 records, but both are administered by the circulation staff independently of the audiovisual department.

Library staff and faculty at Earlham describe both Lilly and Wildman as "reference-oriented libraries." They agree that it is more prudent for Earlham to spend its limited library funds on reference works than on building a large book and periodical collection. This has several important implications for library operations. Since the library does not attempt to acquire everything its diverse community of users will need, it must provide adequate arrangements for borrowing materials from other institutions. Earlham is, therefore, most active in interlibrary loans. During 1976-1977, it borrowed about 2,000 items from other libraries, almost two items per year per student. The library also operates a van which travels twice a week to the larger collection at nearby Miami University, transporting both students and books.

The second implication of the reference orientation is that instruction must be provided on the use of library resources, particularly reference tools. The library states in a recent brochure, ". . . .unless students know how to use the library effectively, the entire program is virtually wasted." Each member of the professional staff, including the head librarian, takes a regular shift at the reference desk, and all but one give in-class instruction on reference services and prepare course bibliographies. Earlham's efforts in providing reference services and teaching students to use these services have gained national attention. With both National Science Foundation and Earlham College support, the library has conducted workshops on bibliographic instruction for librarians and faculty from other colleges and universities throughout the country.

In 1977-1978, Earlham spent nearly $275,000 on library operations. Approximately 51 percent was spent for staff salaries and wages, and 40 percent was spent for materials. Of the materials allocation, 65 percent was for books and 35 percent for periodicals. A substantial portion of funds used to support current periodicals goes to indexing and abstracting services, especially in the sciences. The library spends little on audiovisual materials, purchasing essentially only slides and phonorecords.

In the past five years, overall library expenditures have increased by nearly $30,000, about 12 percent of 1973-1974 expenditures. Most of this increase has been used to supplement staff salaries in response to inflation and to provide access to computer-aided cataloging services. Only $5,000, or about 5 percent of the total materials expenditures of 1973-1974, has been added to acquisitions, certainly not sufficient to offset the impact of book and journal price inflation.

Both the head librarian and the head of technical services take responsibility for preparing the annual budget. During December of each year, the head librarian consults with the provost concerning estimates for the college's fiscal resources. With advice from all library staff, the head librarian prepares a proposed budget, which is forwarded to a faculty budget committee in January. Usually by early spring the next year's budget figures are fixed and remain fairly stable from that point. About 70 percent of the library's funds come from the college's own resources. Supplements come from endowment funds, government grants, Title II funds, book sales, copy-machine income, and fines. Additional funds for both acquisitions and salaries come from the Earlham School of Religion, a graduate theological program located on the Earlham campus and enrolling forty-five students. Since these students use the library extensively, the School of Religion contributes to a portion of one librarian's salary.

The key to understanding collection-development practices at Earlham is found in the close working relationship among students, faculty, and library staff—a relationship perhaps possible only in a small-college environment. All incoming students are given a library skills test; the test is used to assess readiness for the library instruction which is integrated into almost all Earlham courses. New faculty are queried by the library concerning the materials needed to support their instructional programs; this contact occurs long before the faculty member arrives on campus and commences a continuing faculty-library dialog. None of the professional library staff have tenure, but they do have academic appointments, enjoy all faculty privileges, and sit on a number of key faculty committees, including the committee which reviews new course or program proposals.

It is clear that Earlham represents an endpoint on at least one important dimension relevant to collection development in academic libraries, that is, the centrality of the library in the educational milieu of the institution. Use of the library's reference resources is an important and uniformly applied gauge of the performance of both students and faculty. Very few students graduate from Earlham without having learned how to use the library's resources as a natural consequence of their academic progression. In addition, very few faculty attain permanent status without having organized their courses to ensure their students' involvement in the use of the library's reference resources.

Stockton State College

Having commenced its first academic year in 1971, Stockton State College is the youngest of nine colleges in New Jersey. Total expenditures in 1977-1978 were just over $11 million. Stockton presently has an enrollment of 3,823 full-time-equivalent students, and faculty size is 170. The governance of Stockton is vested by statute in a board of trustees which sets overall policies and appoints the president, the chief executive officer. The college is divided into four administrative units, and the library resides within one of these, the Office of Educational Services. The fourteen professionals on the staff have concurrent academic appointments and are eligible for tenure.

Stockton's curriculum is organized in five major divisions: arts and humanities, natural sciences and mathematics, social and behavioral sciences, professional studies, and general studies. Traditional bachelor's-degree programs are offered within the first three divisions. Professional studies includes degree programs in biomedical communications, business studies, information and systems sciences, speech pathology and audiology, nursing, and public health. The bachelor of arts in liberal studies and teacher certification are available through general studies. For the most part, general-studies courses are taken by students in their first two years at Stockton, and these courses fulfill requirements for work outside a student's major area. Some 400 different courses have been offered through general studies, including courses on such topics as Soviet dissidents, human sexuality, dinosaurs, and mechanical drawing. A major curricular emphasis at Stockton is self-directed, independent study. The 777 bachelor's degrees awarded in 1978 were distributed as follows: sciences, 23 percent; social sciences, 66 percent; humanities, 10 percent; other, 1 percent. The largest concentration is in business studies, accounting for one-third of the degrees awarded.

Stockton is located on a 1,600-acre wooded campus in southern New Jersey, near Atlantic City. The college is composed of thirteen buildings alternately arrayed along the sides of a pedestrian gallery. The design has won several national architectural awards. Practically one-third of all Stockton students are from New Jersey counties in close proximity to the college. The male students outnumber the female students by a ratio of approximately 3 to 2.

Stockton's library began operations with limited services during the planning year preceding the college's opening. In the fall of 1970, the library made its first major purchase of materials—the 16,000-volume antiquarian bookstore collection of Joseph A. Kury of Philadelphia. By June 1972, total volume count had risen to 31,000. The collection has since tripled in size. As of July 1978, library holdings at Stockton included some 94,000 bound volumes; and the book collection is growing at the rate of 10,000 volumes per year. The library's collection is designed to support the college's instructional programs.

With few exceptions, library resources and activities are housed in one facility—a 52,000-square-foot, three-story structure. Government documents and media services constitute major portions of this facility. In July 1977, the documents collection exceeded 80,000. The media collection had some 65,000 units, including 60,000 slides, 1,700 phonorecords, 1,300 transparencies, 1,000 audiotapes, 750 films, 500 filmstrips, 400 multimedia kits, and 200 videotapes. The library maintains special facilities, such as listening and film-viewing stations, which allow all media formats to be used within the library. The library also supervises facilities which permit in-house production of a variety of media, including a graphics area, an audio studio, two darkrooms, and a TV studio. The TV studio and one of the darkrooms are located within other buildings of the campus.

The library has automated a number of library functions. Stockton was the first New Jersey state college library to join the Pennsylvania Library Information Network (PALINET), a regional network, to obtain on-line cataloging services from the Ohio College Library Center (OCLC). In September 1976, an automated circulation system was implemented. The reference department now offers on-line data-base searching. Finally, Stockton was the only U.S. library currently using CODOC, a unique system developed in Canada and used by Stockton for bibliographic control of all documents, periodicals, and media materials.

Figure 3-2 illustrates the organizational structure of the library, consisting of three components: technical services, public services, and media services. Within technical services reside acquisitions and cataloging. The recently established position of collection-development librarian is also part of technical services.

Public services includes both reference services and circulation, the latter handling circulation of both book and nonbook materials. Stockton is a partial depository library for selected Atlantic County, New Jersey, and U.S. government publications. This collection is administered by one of the four reference librarians in public services. Interlibrary loan and library instruction, both growing programs at Stockton, are within public services. The library borrowed 4,158 items from other libraries in 1977-1978.

In addition to its involvement in media collection development, media services supervises the use of the college darkrooms and studios. Among its staff are media collection-development and production specialists. A professional librarian heads this unit.

As a state agency, Stockson is supported primarily by funds appropriated by the legislature. Units within the college submit budget requests for each fiscal year. The library has successfully sought a number of

STOCKTON STATE COLLEGE LIBRARY

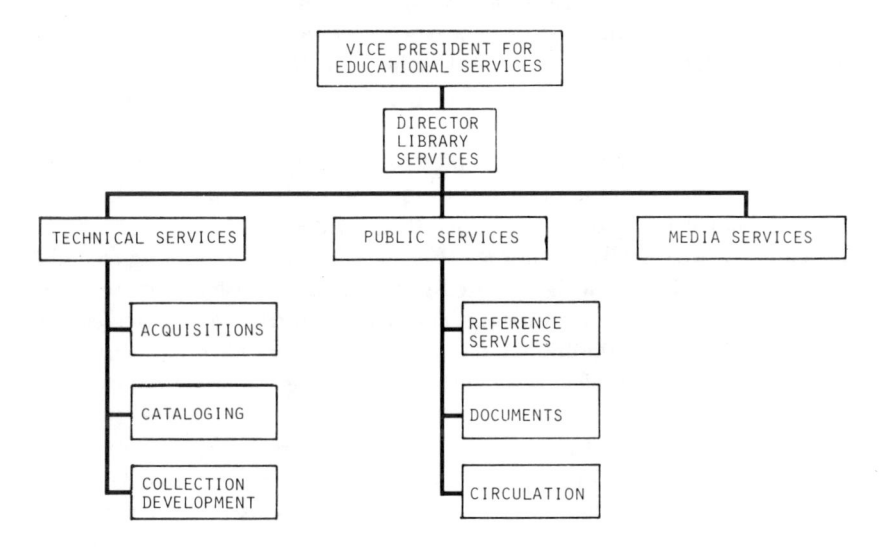

Figure 3-2. Organizational Chart of Stockton State College Library

outside grants. However, these account for only a small fraction of its operating expenses, and the library relies primarily on its annual appropriation. It sometimes receives additional monies from the college administration as the fiscal year proceeds and typically spends these funds on materials. Among items considered for purchase with a recent additional allocation of nearly $60,000 were materials in support of a new teacher-education program, frequently rented films, census materials, slide/tape programs, and general-interest paperbacks.

The total library budget for 1977-1978 was just over $1 million. The salary allocation was 44 percent, and the materials allocation, including binding, was 39 percent of the total budget. The remaining 17 percent of the budget was expanded for operating expenses, including substantial outlays for media-services' equipment purchase, rental, and maintenance.

With the exception of two years when funding throughout the state was limited, the library budget has been increasing steadily since the library's first year of operation. But major portions of each increase were allocated to salaries, and the book budget has remained relatively stable. Although the allocation for current periodicals, indexes, and abstracts has increased by almost 400 percent, the total number of subscriptions has not increased proportionally. The present $100,000 periodicals allocation maintains some 1,600 titles.

Faculty constantly request new periodical subscriptions, and last year the library did add 100 new titles. However, this year the library is attempting to contain further growth. To aid in this endeavor, the staff has initiated a program to evaluate the collection, with the intention of weeding out journals which receive little use. Student workers who maintain the periodical area record the names of journals they reshelve, and library users are requested to note use of an issue by marking slips which have been stapled to journal covers.

Stockton is a new institution, and its library faces many problems not experienced by libraries in older institutions. It is attempting to build a collection responsive to a college in which the priorities of academic programs have not yet been firmly established. Furthermore, it is attempting to build an adequate collection with a limited budget and no base collection from which to start. The latter problem is complicated further by the decreasing purchasing power of the library dollar. These factors have hampered the library's efforts to establish systematic collection-development policies and practices.

However, as a relatively new institution, Stockton has considerable flexibility in developing its library services. The library has been able to implement automated procedures without encountering many of the traumas of change experienced by older institutions. In recent years, nonbook materials have gained wider acceptance as appropriate instructional aids at Stockton. Whereas most older libraries must undergo costly structural modifications to support a new media collection, Stockton's library was expressly designed to support extensive in-library use of media.

Presently, the key to Stockton's collection development is utility. The library is not attempting to build a core general collection—it would rather acquire titles that will be used, not that may be used. Library staff participate in collection development, but the focus of selection activity is on the faculty, who are assumed to be in the best position to choose the titles users will need.

Brown University

Brown University is a privately endowed, nonsectarian institution in Providence, Rhode Island. Founded in 1764, it was the seventh college in the U.S. colonies. Brown first admitted a small group of women in 1891 and subsequently established a separate women's institution, Pembroke College. In 1971 Pembroke merged with the college for undergraduate men, making Brown a fully integrated, coeducational institution.

Although Brown first offered graduate instruction as early as 1887, the major emhasis today remains on the undergraduate programs. In 1977-1978 there were 5,492 undergraduate and 1,442 graduate students.

In the late 1960s, Brown thoroughly revised all its curricula and eliminated all distribution requirements, thereby proliferating a variety of individualized majors and cross-disciplinary concentrations. A wide selection of course offerings, including extradepartmental courses, specialized seminars, and independent study, allow considerable flexibility in all academic programs. In 1977-1978, academic degrees awarded by Brown University were distributed as follows:

	Bachelor's	*Master's*	*Doctoral*
Sciences	30%	30%	60%
Social Sciences	25	28	15
Humanities	36	34	22
Other	9	8	3
Number	1,178	192	192

Of the undergraduate degrees conferred 36 percent were in the humanities, with history and literature being most popular, and 30 percent were in the sciences, with biology being most popular. Sixty percent of all the doctorates are given in the sciences, with one-third in the field of medicine. Since 1973, Brown has offered a specially designed program leading to the M.D. This program was established in order to provide medical education which included the humanities and social sciences. Students may be admitted as first-year students and have the option of completing their undergraduate and medical degrees within seven years. In 1977-1978, sixty-four such degrees were awarded. The new medical program, which places additional demands on the library for materials relevant to medical training, resides within the university's division of biology and medicine and is not associated with an independent medical school.

The university library consists of four facilities. The humanities and social-science collections are located in the John D. Rockefeller, Jr., Library, the largest facility. On one edge of the campus, this seven-story building also houses the library's administrative offices. On the opposite edge of campus is the newest unit, the Sciences Library, which contains the science collections, including the materials for the medical program. The Pembroke Library previously served the instructional programs of Pembroke College. It is now part of the university library, but Pembroke still purchases all its materials with the income from its own endowed funds and receives no university allocation for acquisitions. The Pembroke collection is basically a general collection in the social sciences and the humanities, but it also contains several strong collections in specialized areas. Because of the latter, library staff prefer not to view Pembroke as an undergraduate library; but, for the most part, its collection and clientele are clearly similar to those of other undergraduate libraries.

The fourth and oldest unit in Brown's library system is the John Hay Library. This library, which formerly contained the university's social-science and humanities collections, is adjacent to the Rockefeller Library. Today the John Hay Library contains only special collections, which are numerous. Among its strengths are the Harris Collection of Poetry and Plays; the Abraham Lincoln Collection; one of the largest collections of U.S. sheet music outside the Library of Congress; several important collections of sixteenth- and seventeenth-century scientific papers; about 30,000 broadsides representing a variety of substantive areas; the Henry D. Thoreau Collection; the Whaling Collection; and nearly sixty collections of manuscripts.

In addition to several small departmental collections, Brown University has two special libraries that are not under the direct supervision of the university librarian: The John Carter Brown Library and the Annmary Brown Library. The directors of both these libraries report instead to the dean of the faculty and academic affairs. The John Carter Brown Library has one of the most extensive collections of Americana in the world. It collects materials printed during the Colonial period relevant to the discovery and settlement of the New World. Until recently, the 40,000-volume collection was supported by its original endowment, but since this income no longer covers all costs, the university now contributes significantly to its support.

Profiles of Seven Academic Libraries

The Annmary Brown Memorial Library, also established with an endowment, contains a world-famous collection of incunabula, that are particularly valuable in the areas of medieval and Renaissance studies. Because of increasing cost, the Annmary Brown Library has also recently become more dependent on university funding. At one period, the library was forced to close, but it is now reopened and houses all activities of the Renaissance studies program.

The university library houses over 1.5 million volumes, and there are forty-seven professional librarians on the staff. The holdings of the Rockefeller Library number about 1 million volumes. Printed books in the special collections of the John Hay Library number about 275,000. The Sciences Library houses close to 250,000 volumes, and the Pembroke houses more than 17,000. Expenditures for the system in 1977-1978 totaled $2.7 million. Salaries, wages, and benefits accounted for 60 percent of the total. Operating expenses were 6 percent, and binding was 3 percent. The remaining 31 percent was devoted to acquisitions.

Figure 3-3 portrays the organizational chart for the university library. Reporting directly to the university librarian are four assistant university librarians. One assistant university librarian is responsible for circulation in each of the four library units as well as the systems department. Established in 1972, the systems department provides computer support for a number of

BROWN UNIVERSITY LIBRARIES

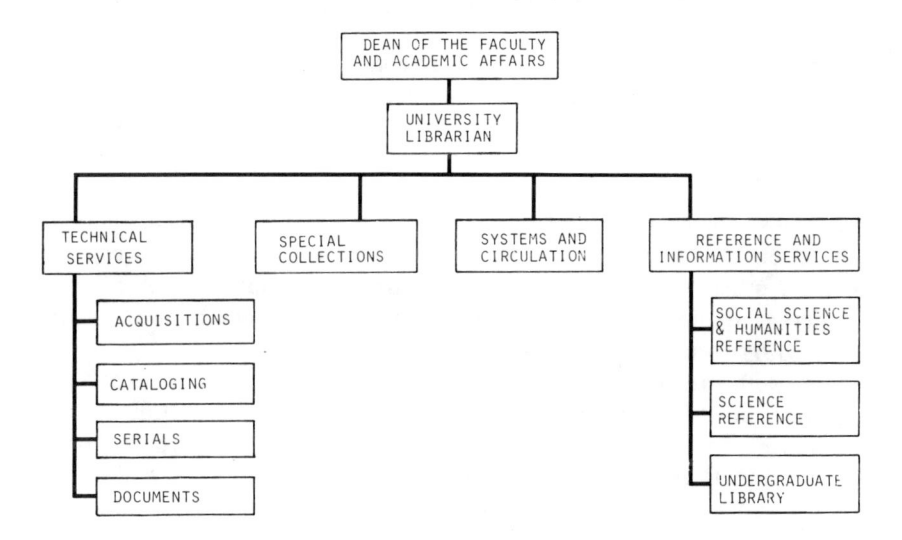

Figure 3-3. Organizational Chart of Brown University Libraries

library activities including acquisitions, fund accounting, reserve books, student payroll, and photocopy billing.

The assistant university librarian for reference and information services is in charge of all reference activities except for those related to the special collections in the John Hay Library. The head of the Pembroke library and the reference librarians in both Rockefeller and Sciences report to the reference and information services librarian. There are nine reference librarians in the Rockefeller and the Sciences. Because of their role in collection development, they are also called *reference selectors*. At Brown, reference librarians are the only persons on the library staff involved in item selection. There are no library staff designated as bibliographers or collection-development officers. Interlibrary loan units exist at two points in the library system, one within the Rockefeller Library and the other within the Sciences Library. These units also report to the assistant university librarian for reference and information services.

The assistant university librarian for technical services supervises systemwide acquisitions and cataloging activities. Although the serials and documents departments report to the technical-services librarian, both departments also include public-services activities, that is, assisting users in locating materials. These public-service activities exist in both the Sciences Library and the Rockefeller Library. The John Hay Library and the Pembroke Library have substantial serials collections, but the serials department does not supervise public access to these collections.

The assistant university librarian for special collections is head of the John Hay Library and supervises six curators and the university archivist, all professional librarians. With the exception of the East Asian Collection, located in the Rockefeller Library, all special collections in the system are housed in the John Hay Library. There is a division of labor among the curators corresponding to the distinctive parts of the special collections, defined by either the subject area or the format of the materials. For example, the curator of the Harris Collection maintains a collection of U.S. poetry and plays, a collection defined by subject area. On the other hand, the curator of broadsides maintains a collection of posters and other documents under four pages in length, a collection defined by format.

As with special collections in most academic libraries, access to and circulation of the John Hay's holdings are restricted. Furthermore, the reference activities of the curators are very different from those of the reference staff in the Rockefeller and Sciences Libraries. For example, most of the requests for reference services directed to the curators come from scholars outside the Brown community, and to respond effectively to such requests usually requires both more time and greater specific substantive expertise than is usually demanded of a reference librarian.

The four units of the university library are part of a unified system; two of the units, though, are more self-directing in certain aspects of their operation. The Pembroke and the John Hay function more independently than the Sciences Library and the Rockefeller Library. Unlike the Rockefeller and the Sciences, both the Pembroke and the John Hay have individuals identified as their heads. The Pembroke's long history of independent operation as well as the fact that its acquisitions and equipment expenses are still supported entirely by dedicated endowments further contributes to its relative autonomy. The John Hay receives no university appropriation for its materials acquisitions; this as well as the unique features of its operation further explains its relative independence.

The budget-making process of the university library begins in the fall of each year. The university librarian first consults with the dean of the faculty and academic affairs and then the faculty library committee, which serves in an advisory capacity. A preliminary budget is proposed and submitted to the president of the university. The budget is divided into three major categories: materials acquisitions, salaries and wages, and operating expenses. The focus of attention in the budget-review process is primarily on acquisitions funds, since the proposed budgets in the other categories are determined, for the most part, by university guidelines.

The president forwards the budget to the academic committee on university planning (ACUP). This committee is composed of elected representatives of faculty and students and appointees from the administration. It serves in an advisory capacity to the president and is the major policy-making body on campus. Its recommendations in recent years have usually been accepted.

As a result of the ACUP review, the library budget typically undergoes some revision. In recent years, this scrutiny has resulted in an increase in the amount of money made available for new materials. Frequently, in the course of its review, the ACUP may request the university librarian and other library staff members to appear before them to discuss the budget. Both the ACUP and the university librarian forward their final recommendations for the budget to the dean of the faculty and academic affairs, who in turn forwards them to the president.

Brown has a somewhat unusual set of diverse sources for its acquisitions funds, which have undergone some important changes in recent years. The allocation for acquisitions has four components. The first is called the library appropriation, and these funds are allocated from general university revenues. The second component is called current restricted funds (CRF), an aggregation of donations to the university that is made available to the library for acquisitions. These funds are typically received during the course of the fiscal year. The third component consists of endowed funds earmarked for library materials, and the fourth is the dedicated fund for the medical-program acquisitions.

Since the final amount of donations received by the university in any one year can never be predicted accurately, CRF are considered "soft monies." This type of money was more abundant and predictable in the past when Brown University was receiving more generous gifts from many supporters. But in recent years, Brown, as well as many other private institutions, has not been the object of such generous support. Indeed, the decrease in CRF has caused a minor fiscal crisis at Brown University. As a result, the university librarian has convinced the administration that the CRF component must be reduced to introduce greater stability into the library's expectations of sums available for new materials. Thus, the 1976-1977 proposed budget had over 30 percent of the acquisitions funds from CRF, but in the budget for 1977-1978, CRF were reduced to 11.5 percent.

Library acquisitions budgets at Brown, as elsewhere, are being rapidly eroded by the constantly increasing costs of books and periodicals. The impact of inflation on the Brown library system has been severe. In 1970, total acquisitions for Brown amounted to about $604,000; in 1972, about $507,000; and in 1974, about $602,000. During those years, there was a drastic and steady decrease in the number of volumes added to the collection: in 1970, 46,000 volumes; in 1972, 32,000; and in 1974, about 28,000. This discouraging decrease has prompted the university librarian and the faculty to lobby for more support for library acquisitions. The situation at Brown has improved lately. In 1977-1978 almost 40,000 volumes were added. Nevertheless, the acquisitions budget is still far below what the librarians feel appropriate to build library support for new academic programs as well as maintain adequate support for continuing programs.

The Pennsylvania State University

Established as the Farmers' High School in 1855, Penn State was designated as the commonwealth's land-grant institution in 1874. Today it is the largest university in Pennsylvania and includes the main campus in University Park, seventeen two-year commonwealth campuses, a small graduate center in Radnor, a four-year campus in Erie, a campus with limited graduate programs in the state capital, and a medical school in Hershey. In 1977-1978 the total operating budget for all Penn State units was $263 million. The university is governed by a board of trustees composed of elected representatives from the alumni association and various business and professional groups throughout the commonwealth.

Over 200 undergraduate- and graduate-degree programs are offered in the following areas: agriculture; arts and architecture; business administration; earth and mineral sciences; education; engineering; health, physical education, and recreation; human development; and liberal arts and sciences. Academic degrees awarded at University Park in 1977-1978 were distributed as follows:

	Bachelor's	*Master's*	*Doctoral*
Sciences	38%	36%	46%
Social Sciences	51	54	46
Humanities	8	9	8
Other	3	1	—
Number	7,545	1,260	340

It is clear from these data that the emphasis at Penn State is on the undergraduate level. Engineering and agriculture account for 55 percent of the undergraduate science degrees, and business administration and education account for 53 percent of the social-science undergraduate degrees. At the graduate level, education, engineering, and the physical sciences are the most common fields of study, reflecting a pattern that is characteristic of many land-grant institutions.

The Pennsylvania State University libraries now contain over 2 million volumes, 1.5 million microforms, and 23,000 continuing serials. In 1977-1978, they served 52,584 students, of whom 48,796 were undergraduate and 3,798 were graduate students. Faculty size was 3,070. At University Park alone, there were 30,437 undergraduates, 3,557 graduate students, and 1,662 faculty members. There were a total of 102 professional librarians employed by the university libraries, and 74 of these were on the main campus.

Both the graduate program at the state capital and the medical school at Hershey have libraries with budgets that are separately administered. But the libraries of the remaining nineteen campuses and the libraries of the main campus at University Park are budgeted as a system and are the administrative responsibility of the dean of the university libraries, who is located at University Park. Volume count on the main campus at University Park is about 1.5 million; the other nineteen campuses under the dean together house about 600,000 volumes, ranging from 15,000 at Radnor to almost 70,000 at Erie. The University Park collections are strongest in the fields which the university has traditionally emphasized—agriculture, engineering, and the sciences. The seventeen two-year campus libraries are primarily oriented toward support of first- and second-year undergraduate curricula, particularly in technical and scientific fields.

The bulk of library holdings at University Park is the Fred Lewis Pattee

Library. The Pattee collection of 1,250,000 volumes includes the social-science and humanities library resources. In addition, Pattee houses maps, government documents, special collections, a discrete collection serving agriculture and the biological sciences, and another serving the fine arts. Another 220,000 volumes at University Park are distributed among seven major branches of Pattee: a physical-science branch containing 61,000 volumes, an earth-and-mineral-sciences branch of 58,000 volumes, an engineering branch of 45,000 volumes, a mathematics branch of 23,000 volumes, an architecture reading room of 12,000 volumes, and two small undergraduate collections serving dormitories. Over fifty smaller collections are located throughout the campus in departments and research institutes; these are administered by the departments and partially supported by the library.

As shown in figure 3-4, the dean of university libraries reports to the provost and has responsibility for all units in the system: technical services, public services, administration, collection development, the campus libraries, and library instruction. Technical services includes systemwide acquisitions and cataloging. Serials for University Park are ordered by the serials department, but serials for the campus libraries are ordered by the

THE PENNSLVANIA STATE UNIVERSITY STATE LIBRARIES

```
                    PROVOST
                       |
              DEAN OF UNIVERSITY
                  LIBRARIES
                       |
   ┌──────────┬────────┼────────┬──────────┬──────────┐
TECHNICAL  PUBLIC  ADMINISTRATION & COLLECTION COMMONWEALTH LIBRARY
SERVICES   SERVICES    SYSTEMS   DEVELOPMENT  CAMPUS    INSTRUCTION
                                              LIBRARIES
   │          │           │          │
ACQUISITIONS HUMANITIES & BUSINESS
             SOCIAL SCIENCES ADMINISTRATION
             SCIENCE &
             TECHNOLOGY
CATALOGING                  PERSONNEL
             CIRCULATION    ADMINISTRATION
             INTER-LIBRARY
             LOAN           COMPUTER
SERIALS                     SYSTEMS
             SPECIAL
             COLLECTION
```

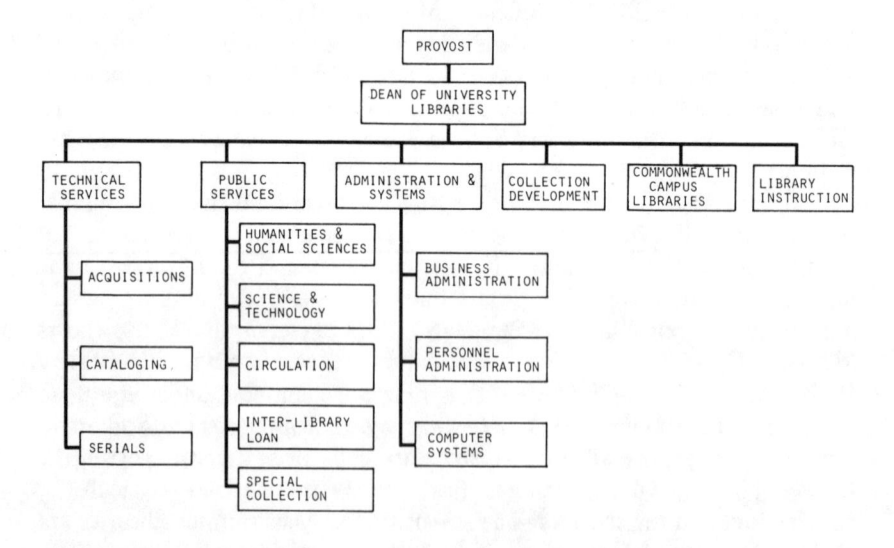

Figure 3-4. Organizational Chart of The Pennsylvania State University Libraries

acquisitions department. In addition to its role in technical services, the serials department administers a periodical reading room in Pattee.

At University Park, science and technology public-service units are administered separately from the humanities and social-science units. All science branches, including the agriculture and life-science collection in Pattee, are part of the science-and-technology department. The head of the humanities and social-science department is responsible for the fine-arts library; the documents, maps, and microform departments; an eight-member reference staff serving the humanities and social sciences; and the architecture reading room. All units within the humanities and social-science section are located in Pattee.

Public services also include the special-collections, interlibrary-loan, and circulation-services departments. Interlibrary loans handles both lending and borrowing services, which in 1977-1978 were 16,687 and 5,089, respectively. Stack control, reserves, and photoduplication in Pattee are part of the circulation department. In the branches at University Park and on the campuses, circulation services is administered locally.

An associate dean for administration supervises business and personnel units as well as the library's developing computer systems. In addition, the associate dean has responsibility for preparing the overall library budget for the dean's review and for monitoring systemwide expenditures. The associate dean is, therefore, intimately involved in the daily activities of all units of the Penn State libraries.

The collection-development coordinator holds a recently created position which reflects the library's growing desire for more rational and effective collection-development practices. A collection-development committee, chaired by the coordinator and consisting of librarians from several departments, is supervising the production of collection-development policy statements as well as a count of library holdings in substantive areas defined by Library of Congress categories. It will also prepare a five-year plan of collection-development goals.

The coordinator of commonwealth campus libraries is responsible for overall supervision of the nineteen campus libraries. Technical services and intrasystem library loans are provided centrally from University Park. Public services and collection development are managed locally and monitored by the coordinator. Librarians at the campuses report to both the senior academic officer on their campuses and the dean of university libraries through the coordinator.

One professional librarian and several part-time student workers make up the administrative staff of the library instruction unit. The teaching staff are drawn from other units throughout the library. Among the academic libraries included in this project, Penn State is unique in having a separate department charged with the mission of library instruction. The department is responsible for all credited instruction in library studies at all locations, although the provision of teaching time and scheduling of courses is a local responsibility.

Penn State operates on a fiscal year running from July 1 to June 30. In October of each year, the university administration prepares a preliminary budget request for the institution and by November submits it to the governor's office. At the same time, based on financial expectations, each **academic and administrative unit is asked to submit a budget request for** the next year. In the case of academic units, including the libraries, these requests are analyzed by the budget office and reviewed by the provost's advisory budget task force, which also conducts hearings for each unit during January and February. The governor presents a proposed budget during February for consideration by the state legislature. From the results of the budget-review hearings and the likely state budget, the provost recommends to the president a specific apportionment of the next year's budget. At this stage, the various academic units are advised of their likely operating budget for the next year. If any changes can be made, they are then negotiated. In May the various units are asked to prepare an initial operating budget for the next fiscal year. If the legislature has not acted or appears likely to decrease the appropriation, this initial operating budget may carry several restrictions on hiring or other expenditures.

In most of the last twelve years, the Pennsylvania State Legislature has been excessively slow in approving the university budget, which is a nonpreferred item and must await the prior approval of the general state budget before action is taken. In 1977-1978, funds were not appropriated until November, almost five months into the new fiscal year. Not only did this delay cause a great deal of uncertainty concerning available resources, but it cost the university several thousand dollars a day in interest payments on money borrowed to meet operating expenses.

In spite of the very undesirable fiscal uncertainty that occurs at the beginning of each fiscal year, the Penn State library frequently experiences a positive gain as the fiscal year closes. These windfalls are usually salary savings from the library's budget or transfers from the university administration. However, no funds may be carried forward to the next fiscal year; thus there is frequently a rush to expend funds at the last minute. The year-end supplements occur fairly regularly and are now more or less anticipated. Many librarians confidently plan for some additional funds beyond those budgeted each year. In fact, the library sometimes reports two separate sets of figures for each fiscal year—funds budgeted and funds expended; the latter are informally defined as "budgeted-plus windfalls."

In 1977-1978, total expenditures for The Pennsylvania State University libraries, which include University Park, the two-year campuses, and the campuses of Erie and Radnor, were $7,077,000. Of that amount, 77 percent supported the libraries at University Park, with the remaining 23 percent supporting the libraries at the other campuses. Of the University Park budget, 61 percent was used for salaries and wages, 10 percent for operating expenses, and the remaining 29 percent for library materials and binding. The $1.4 million spent for materials at University Park added nearly 48,000 volumes to the collection.

The inflexibility of the Penn State library budget is a paramount concern of the library administration. Money available for acquisitions has remained relatively stable over the past few years; but as the dollar's purchasing power has gone down, fewer and fewer dollars were left after paying for subscriptions and blanket orders. In fact, on the first day of the 1977-1978 fiscal year, the library had committed nearly 75 percent of its budget on subscriptions and blanket or approval plans. Library staff feel that essential materials are not being purchased because of the constraints on their discretionary spending.

Several activities of the collection-development committee will have an impact on this problem. Under the direction of the head of the serials department, an effort is being made to identify serials titles for possible cancellation. In 1977-1978, 511 serials subscriptions were terminated. In addition, thorough reviews of the appropriateness of materials received under approval plans are being undertaken with the hope of releasing funds budgeted to these plans. Also, the committee is working with the systems development department to determine what data may become available from scheduled automation projects that will be helpful in determining collection-development policies and practices.

Because of the practical problems involved in gathering data from the nineteen different units under the dean's supervision which are located outside University Park, collection-development policies and practices were studied on the main campus only. Except as noted below, all further discussion of Penn State in this book is limited to library activities at University Park.

The University of North Carolina, Chapel Hill

The University of North Carolina, Chapel Hill, opened its doors to students in 1795 as the nation's first state university. In 1931, it merged with the North Carolina College for Women at Greensboro and the North Carolina State College of Agriculture and Engineering at Raleigh to form the University of North Carolina. In 1978, the University of North Carolina (UNC) had sixteen campuses and a total operating budget of $174 million. Each campus is headed by a chancellor and operates independently. The main campus, Chapel Hill, is the only unit included in this study.

In the 1977-1978 academic year, enrollment at UNC Chapel Hill was

18,844, of whom 13,587 were undergraduate and 5,257 were graduate students. The university maintains a faculty of 1,853. All first- and second-year students, except those in the School of Pharmacy and in the dental-hygiene curriculum, are part of the General College. The curriculum of the General College prepares students for continuing work within one of some fifty baccalaureate-level programs. A full complement of master's and doctoral programs is offered by the graduate school. Professional programs include business, dentistry, education, journalism, law, library science, medicine, nursing, pharmacy, public health, and social work. Programs in both agriculture and engineering are not at Chapel Hill, but in Raleigh. Academic degrees awarded at Chapel Hill in 1977-1978 were distributed as follows:

	Bachelor's	*Master's*	*Doctoral*
Sciences	16%	13%	34%
Social Sciences	62	70	38
Humanities	18	17	27
Other	4	—	1
Number	2,835	896	271

Sixty-two percent of the undergraduate degrees were in the social sciences, including business and education. Almost 40 percent of the doctorates are also in the social sciences.

There are three administratively independent library organizations on the campus: the Academic Affairs Library, with nearly 2 million volumes; the Law Library, with about 181,000 volumes; and the Health Affairs Library, with some 155,000 volumes. The director of the Law Library reports to the provost through the dean of the school of law. The director of the Health Affairs Library reports to the chancellor through the vice chancellor of health services. The university librarian, director of the Academic Affairs Library, reports to the provost.

We studied only the Academic Affairs Library. Again, we remind the reader that the data reported here will be different from statistical summaries which include data for the law and medical libraries. The great bulk of the Academic Affairs Library collection, 1.4 million volumes, is housed in the Louis Round Wilson Library building. Ten departmental libraries maintain more than 350,000 volumes of the Academic Affairs collection. The Robert B. House Undergraduate Library, also part of Academic Affairs, has some 93,000 volumes. Professional librarians employed in Academic Affairs number eighty.

The Wilson Library serves primarily the social sciences and the humanities. Special collections in Wilson include materials relating to North Carolina or written by North Carolinians, a rare-book collection, and materials relating to Southern history. Department libraries serve, for the most part, the sciences and fine arts. Exceptions are collections in library science, public law, state and local government, and city and regional planning. The resources at Wilson Library and the department libraries are research-centered and used for the most part by upper-division undergraduates, graduate students, and faculty.

Supporting the curriculum of the General College is the primary goal of the undergraduate library. Emphasis in the collection is on languages, literature, history, and the social sciences. Volumes in these subject areas make up approximately 75 percent of the collection. The sciences account for less than 10 percent of the holdings.

The faculty at UNC Chapel Hill are actively involved in the operation of the Academic Affairs Library. Fifteen members, elected by faculty and representing all divisions of the university, sit on the library administrative board. Together with the university librarian, the board formulates all policies governing the library.

The Wilson Library houses the administrative and business offices,

THE UNIVERSITY OF NORTH CAROLINA, CHAPEL HILL, LIBRARIES

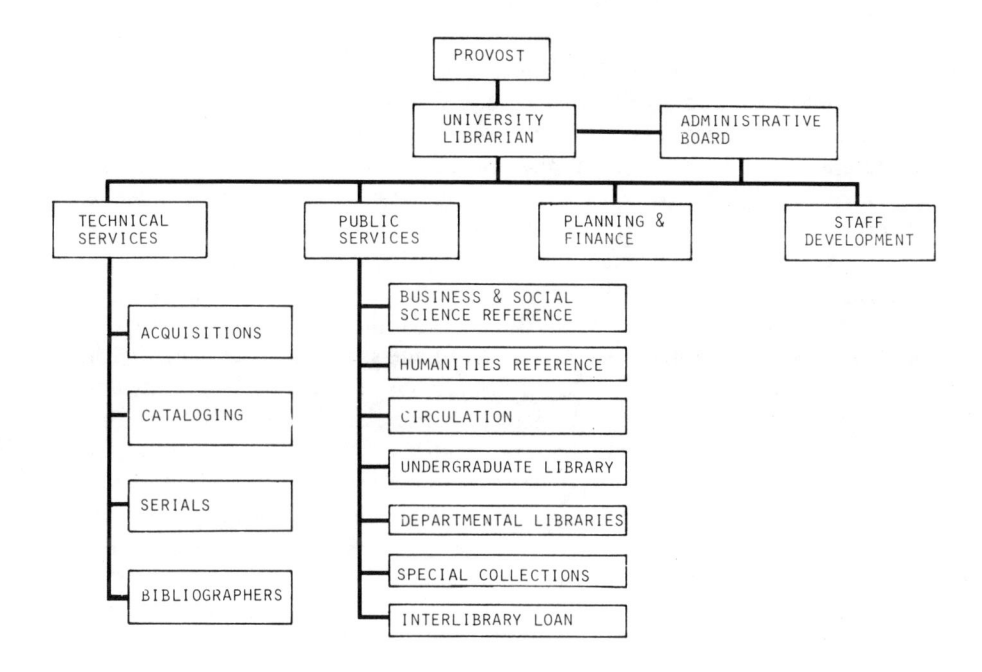

Figure 3-5. Organizational Chart of The University of North Carolina, Chapel Hill, Libraries

technical services, and humanities and social-sciences reference rooms. Figure 3-5 illustrates the interrelationships of these and other activities. Four administrative units report to the university librarian: technical services, public services, planning and finance, and staff development.

With few exceptions, library-wide acquisitions and cataloging are performed by staff within the technical-services division. Exceptions to this occur when the tasks involved require specialized skills. For example, the music library, a departmental library, retains two catalogers primarily responsible for scores and phonorecords which present special problems. The serials department, also within technical services, coordinates system-wide selection and binding of serials. It also plays a public-service role in that it maintains unbound current issues of serials for use in a periodicals reading room in Wilson.

The library's bibliographers are located in technical services. There are six bibliographers: a chief bibliographer, two subject bibliographers (humanities and social science), and three area bibliographers (Asian, Latin American, and Slavic). They are broadly charged with coordinating the university's overall collection-development program and with developing shared and cooperative programs with other universities. Items acquired by the bibliographers are typically most relevant to the humanities and social sciences and are housed in the Wilson Library.

Public services includes two reference departments: humanities and business administration/social sciences. Both are responsible for identifying and acquiring bibliographic tools that contribute to the research holdings in a number of areas and subjects. All department libraries and the undergraduate library report to the associate librarian for public services, as does the interlibrary services center. Annually UNC Chapel Hill lends 12,000 to 13,000 items and borrows less than 3,000 items.

In recent years, the Academic Affairs Library has enjoyed substantial increases in annual budget allocations, owed largely to the state's attempt to add to the library's resources. This development program began in 1973 and ended in 1978. Throughout this period, budgets were supplemented with allocations determined by enrollments at various degree levels. The state appropriation in 1975-1976 was 11 percent higher than in 1974-1975, and in 1976-1977 it was 13 percent higher than in 1975-1976. The books and serials budget received 48 percent of the 1975-1976 increase and 39 percent of the 1976-1977 increase. Salaries, on the other hand, received 20 percent of the 1975-1976 increase and 40 percent of the 1976-1977 increase. These additional resources are aiding the library in coping with the impact of inflation on salaries and acquisitions. The library was able to add over 87,000 new volumes to the collection in 1977-1978. It also added 818 new serials titles and terminated only 316 subscriptions.

Largely as a result of the state's biennial fiscal schedule, the library's state allocation in any given year is perceived as composed of two parts: a continuation budget and the increase over last year's budget. An administrative council, composed of the university librarian and the associate and assistant librarians, distributes monies within all budget categories except materials. The allocation of the materials budget is the responsibility of the library administrative board.

In 1977-1978, total Academic Affairs Library expenditures amounted to $5.2 million. Of this total, 59 percent was expended on salaries, wages, and benefits; 34 percent, on books, serials, and binding; and the remaining 7 percent, on operating expenses. In addition to the state allocation, the library receives approximately $250,000 from a variety of other sources, including some sixty trust funds, a number of which are earmarked for the maintenance of special collections. A recent addition to the annual budget is a substantial allocation derived from overhead on research grants awarded to the Chapel Hill campus. In 1977-1978, this allocation was $105,000. These funds have been applied to the purchase of titles noted in departmental "desiderata lists."

Through a standing budget committee, the library administrative board allocates monies available for books and serials publications among three general categories—books, standing orders, and serials—and then further distributes each of these allocations among some sixty-six materials funds. Members of the budget committee include board members and the chief bibliographer, the latter playing an instrumental role in the decisions that are made.

At UNC Chapel Hill, faculty involvement in item selection is a long-standing tradition as well as a source of some pride. In 1977-1978 over half of the money budgeted for books was placed in funds administered by faculty. But an effort several years ago to review the entire collection and produce desiderata lists for each materials fund prompted the formulation and adoption of a new policy for allocating these funds. This new policy, which was approved by the library administrative board, took effect on March 1, 1978, and transferred to library control over three-fourths of the money formerly placed in faculty-controlled book funds. Item selection for all new imprints throughout the system is now the primary responsibility of the bibliographers and the department librarians. Faculty have primary responsibility for selection of retrospective materials. This is a most significant change in policy, and we suspect that many faculty neither perceived nor understood all its implications at the time of its adoption. It surely represents an important change, one that will dramatically affect both collection-development practices and, in turn, the content of the Academic Affairs Library collection.

University of Wisconsin, Madison

The University of Wisconsin is administered by a board of regents and supported primarily by the state. The University of Wisconsin, Madison, is the oldest and largest of the fifteen-unit state university system. Founded in 1848 as a land-grant institution, the Madison campus in 1977-1978 had 25,604 undergraduates, 7,505 graduate students, and 2,236 faculty members. The total operating budget last year was $363 million. Madison has a full complement of undergraduate- and graduate-degree programs, and it supports professional schools in agriculture, business, education, engineering, law, library science, nursing, and social work.

Academic degrees awarded in 1977-1978 were distributed as follows:

	Bachelor's	*Master's*	*Doctoral*
Sciences	34%	34%	49%
Social Sciences	51	54	34
Humanities	14	11	17
Other	1	1	—
Number	4,424	2,058	657

Of the undergraduate degrees awarded, 51 percent are in the social sciences, which includes education, and 34 percent are in the sciences. The same predominance of the sciences and social sciences prevails in graduate degrees, a pattern commonly found in many land-grant institutions.

In June 1978, the central library facility of the Madison campus, Memorial Library, and its fourteen branches housed approximately 2.8 million volumes and employed eighty-nine professional librarians. Many specialized collections are administered independently of the Memorial Library system: the Law School Library, with approximately 195,000 volumes; the Health Sciences Library, with approximately 169,000 volumes; and over 100 smaller collections maintained by individual departments and research institutes. Total collection size for Wisconsin, Madison, is 3.2 million. This book focuses on Memorial Library and its fourteen branches, which together make up the general library system. Again, it should be pointed out that the data reported here, which exclude the law and medical libraries, vary substantially from the data reported in the annual statistical summaries produced by the Association of Research Libraries.

Memorial Library contains the university's main holdings in the humanities and social sciences. Memorial also maintains a general reference collection. A unique feature of the library is its cooperative arrangement with the Wisconsin State Historical Society (WSHS). Through this arrangement, the university community has access to the WSHS collection, thus relieving the Memorial Library of collection responsibility for the history of the American continent. This arrangement is convenient for users of Memorial since the WSHS building is immediately adjacent to the library.

The branch libraries maintain collections in the natural sciences, mathematics, engineering, agriculture, business, fine arts, and social work. The college library, also a branch of the general library system, houses both the circulating and reserve undergraduate collections. Unlike most academic libraries, Wisconsin maintains a substantial permanent reserve collection of approximately 55,000 volumes.

Wisconsin, Madison, is particularly interesting because of the decentralization of library activities and resources. This is a relatively recent phenomenon. Previous library administrations officially prohibited the creation of new branch libraries within the general library system. In response, increasingly larger shares of instructional funds were converted into independent, departmental collections. After the official policy changed, branches grew in both size and number. At a rate of two to three a year, formerly independent departmental libraries are now being incorporated into the general library system. When a library joins the system, its entire collection is recataloged and added to the union listing. Thereafter, the system provides centralized acquisitions, cataloging, and processing services. This historical pattern for the development of the general library system accounts in large measure for the residual autonomy of its various units.

As shown in figure 3-6, the director of the general library system is responsible to the chancellor of the University of Wisconsin, Madison, who, in turn, reports to the president of the statewide system. The general library system is divided into two sections—Memorial and fourteen branches. Technical services, which includes acquisitions, serials processing, original cataloging, and MARC (computer-supported cataloging), is organized within one department. Circulation and reference services are separate departments. There is no director of Memorial Library per se; the heads of technical services, reference services, and circulation report immediately to the director.

Nine bibliographers are included among the staff in reference services. Their subject or area responsibilities are social studies, humanities (European), humanities (British-American), history of science, Ibero-American, Slavic, South and South East Asia, East Asia, and Africa-Middle East. Within their areas of specialization, these bibliographers select titles appropriate for housing in Memorial Library. In addition, they provide reference services and liaison with faculty. Many of the bibliographers have doctoral degrees in fields related to their bibliographic responsibilities, and some hold joint academic appointments in both the library and an academic department.

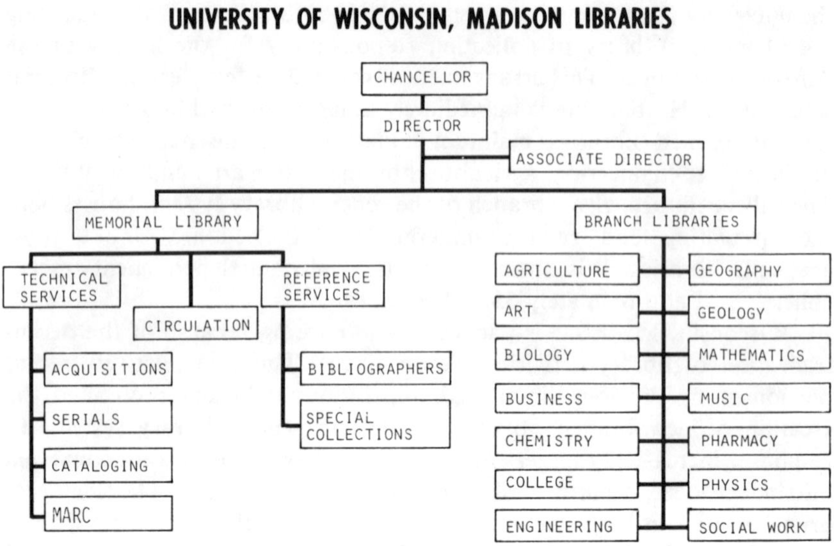

UNIVERSITY OF WISCONSIN, MADISON LIBRARIES

```
                        CHANCELLOR
                            |
                        DIRECTOR
                            |────────ASSOCIATE DIRECTOR
            ┌───────────────┴───────────────┐
      MEMORIAL LIBRARY                 BRANCH LIBRARIES
   ┌────────┬────────┐            ┌──────────┬──────────┐
 TECHNICAL  │    REFERENCE      AGRICULTURE──GEOGRAPHY
 SERVICES   │    SERVICES       ART──────────GEOLOGY
        CIRCULATION             BIOLOGY──────MATHEMATICS
 ACQUISITIONS──BIBLIOGRAPHERS   BUSINESS─────MUSIC
 SERIALS───────SPECIAL          CHEMISTRY────PHARMACY
               COLLECTIONS      COLLEGE──────PHYSICS
 CATALOGING                     ENGINEERING──SOCIAL WORK
 MARC
```

Figure 3-6. Organizational Chart of University of Wisconsin, Madison, Libraries

The branch libraries, forming the second major division within the general library system, are portrayed to the right in figure 3-6. The head of the college library currently serves as the branch library coordinator. All technical services for the branches are performed by the technical-services department in Memorial. Reference and circulation are handled independently by each branch.

There is one additional activity, the Wisconsin interlibrary loan service (WILS), located in Memorial Library, which is not shown on the organizational chart since it operates independently of the general library system. In 1972 WILS was established to facilitate the sharing of library resources throughout the state and to avoid unnecessary duplication of collections. It now includes 49 academic libraries, 350 public libraries, 30 state-agency libraries, and 1,200 school libraries. The University of Wisconsin, Madison, is the largest supplier of materials in WILS, filling almost 74,000 requests in 1977-1978, at an average cost of $2 per item. Patterned after a similar system in Minnesota (MINITEX), WILS now has a cost-free exchange agreement with MINITEX. Although the general library system serves primarily the research activities of its faculty, it must also collect materials to satisfy the needs of the members of WILS.

The University of Wisconsin operates on a biennial budget cycle. For the past several years, the library director has been advised by the chancellor, well before the beginning of a new fiscal year, of the funds allocated to the general library system for the next fiscal year. The appropriations tend to be viewed as increases or cuts from the previous fiscal year. Although it is part of a publicly supported institution, the general library system enjoys a rather stable budgetary environment. With perhaps the exception of an additional allocation from the chancellor's office as the close of the fiscal year approaches, few changes are made during the fiscal year. This stability allows for more effective resource allocation and, in turn, more considered item selection. In 1977-1978, Madison was able to add 109,265 volumes to the collection. In addition, the library initiated 2,559 new serials titles, while terminating 813 subscriptions. Both the biennial budget system and the comparative fiscal strength of the state of Wisconsin account for this unusual position among large academic research libraries.

In 1977-1978, total expenditures of the general library system were just under $6.5 million; and $1.7 million, or 27 percent, was used for library materials. Fifty-four percent of the monies spent on library materials was consumed by continuing commitments to serials subscriptions.

In any library system with a number of semi-independent branch units, collection development can be described as decentralized. Collection development in the general library system at Madison is no exception. But in recent years, the library has made changes which have further decentralized its collection-development activities, particularly in the area of responsibility for funds expended and policy formation. In the past, serials ordered for the Memorial Library were supported by a general serials fund; presently the library is immersed in the task of assigning titles on Memorial's current subscription list and monies which support them to appropriate bibliographers, ultimately distributing the responsibility of expending the general fund among the bibliographers. Librarywide blanket orders have been eliminated and replaced with more specific contracts between vendors and bibliographers. It is intended that this practice will result in more careful monitoring of the appropriateness of titles received. Both the branch librarians and the bibliographers now play a more active role in decisions concerning the distribution of materials funds among them. Each has prepared a formal statement of collection-development responsibilities. Among other things, it is intended that these statements will provide data to rationalize further the fund-allocation process.

University of California, Los Angeles

The University of California, Los Angeles (UCLA), is the second largest unit in the nine-campus university system. In 1919 UCLA was founded as the "southern branch" of the University of California. Its undergraduate enrollment in 1977-1978 was 20,193, and its graduate enrollment was 11,560. The University of California, Los Angeles, comprises a variety of schools, including architecture, dentistry, education, engineering, fine arts, law, library science, management, medicine, nursing, public health, and social welfare. Faculty number 2,313. The University of California, Los Angeles, contains a vast network of organized research units, including such facilities as the Institute of Geophysics and Space Physics, the Molecular Biology Institute, the Brain Research Institute, the Latin America Studies Center, the Institute for Social Research, and the Asian-American Studies Center. Total operating expenditures for UCLA in 1977-1978 were approximately $438 million.

Academic degrees awarded in 1977-1978 were distributed as follows:

	Bachelor's	*Master's*	*Doctoral*
Sciences	36%	31%	68%
Social Sciences	40	50	24
Humanities	20	18	8
Other	4	1	—
Number	4,446	2,284	766

Popular undergraduate majors at UCLA are the social and natural sciences; in fact, 76 percent of the undergraduate degrees are in these fields, with political-science and biology majors especially prevalent. Graduate degrees are concentrated in health sciences and business administration.

Aside from a number of departmental reading rooms, all library units on the UCLA campus are part of a unified library system designated as the University Library. The University Library comprises nineteen units, which together house almost 4 million volumes. This includes the large collections of the health sciences and the law libraries. Therefore, the data reported for UCLA are not comparable with either North Carolina or Wisconsin, where the medical and law libraries were not studied. The largest single collection is that associated with the University Research Library (URL). This collection of about 2,200,000 items is basically a research collection in the humanities and the social sciences. The URL also houses a general reference collection. The college library, another unit in the system, maintains an undergraduate collection of about 200,000 volumes. Its strengths are in the social sciences and humanities. The remaining seventeen library units can be classified as specialized libraries. For the most part, this group consists of libraries primarily serving particular departments or schools. Together they have more than 1.6 million volumes, although they vary considerably in the size of their collections. The largest collection is in the biomedical library, which contains more than 350,000 volumes; the smallest is that found in theater arts, about 6,000 volumes. The nineteen library units are housed in seventeen buildings, thus spreading the library system to all parts of the campus. There are 155 professional librarians employed at UCLA.

The Clark is the only library in the system not formally under the administrative direction of the university librarian. It is a special-collections library emphasizing English culture from 1640 to 1750. Clark is governed by a library committee appointed by the chancellor. Committee members are UCLA faculty, and the chancellor chairs the committee. Clark has both a director and a Clark librarian, the latter acting as the administrative head. The collection and an endowment were bequeathed to UCLA in 1934, and for many years the fund was sufficient to support Clark's entire operation. However, in recent years the endowment income has not been adequate to cover the library's costs; hence UCLA has allocated funds for professional salaries and maintenance of the physical plant. Endowment income is used for collection development, support of visiting-professor fellowships, nonprofessional staff salaries, and the Clark's publication programs.

As can be seen in figure 3-7, the structure of the University Library includes the now-familar separation of technical, here depicted as technical and bibliographic product services, and public services, designated as

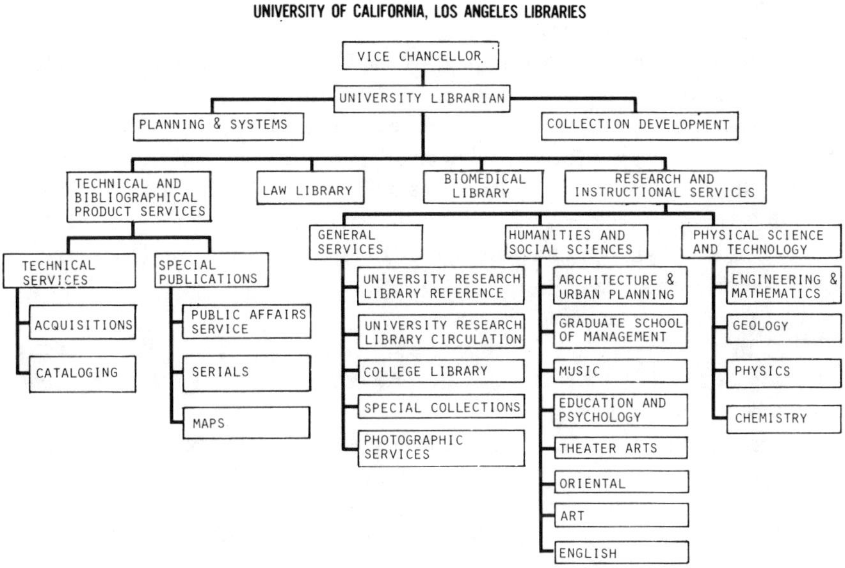

Figure 3-7. Organizational Chart of University of California, Los Angeles, California

research and instructional services. The directors of the law and biomedical libraries report directly to the university librarian. The remaining branches report to various intermediate administrators. With one exception, all these branch libraries are within research and instructional services, with the physical-science branch libraries in one group and humanities and social-sciences libraries in another. The physical-science group reports to the head of research and instructional services through a coordinator of the four libraries. At the time of our study there was no similar coordinator of the humanities and social-sciences group. It should be noted that included among the humanities and social-sciences libraries is a small library associated with the university's elementary school. This library exists solely to support the instructional activities of the laboratory school within the School of Education. Because it is sufficiently different in its collection, staff, and activities from all other library units at UCLA, we decided to exclude it from study.

The last group of units within research and instructional services is the general-services group. Except for the college library, all units within this group are departments of the University Research Library. The reference, circulation, special-collection, and photographic activities of the branch libraries are not part of the general-services section, but reside organizationally within the branch libraries of which they are a part. The University Research Library has no director. Rather, the heads of URL's reference, circulation, special-collection, and photographic services report to the head of research and instructional services.

The technical-services component of the University Library, designated technical and bibliographical product services, includes the acquisitions and cataloging departments, as noted in figure 3-7. Although housed in URL, the departments extend their services to other libraries on campus as well as to URL units. But acquisitions and cataloging at UCLA are not completely centralized. Major exceptions include the law library and the biomedical library, each of which maintains independent acquisitions and cataloging departments. Other exceptions include the Oriental Library, the English reading room, and the Clark Library.

The three units within the special-publications group handle materials requiring acquisitions and cataloging procedures that are quite different from those appropriate for books. Furthermore, the number of items they must process and provide access to in a given period greatly exceeds the number of items handled by other library units. These three units each have a public-service component; but because of the special character of the materials they acquire and maintain, the units are organizationally located within the technical-services component of the library. Public-affairs service and the serials department are housed within URL, but the map library is a branch library, the only branch which reports to technical and bibliographical product services. Public-affairs service is the library's documents department. In addition to government publications, the service collects nongovernment publications produced by domestic and foreign organizations representing a range of political and social activities, as well as documents produced by university and independent study centers.

The serials department extends its processing activities to library units beyond the URL. But, like cataloging and acquisitions activities, serial processing activities are not totally centralized. Those serial processing activities handled by the serials department include ordering of serial titles, payment of invoices, and receipt and distribution of subscriptions. In addition, the serials department negotiates and monitors most foreign exchanges. Serials cataloging is handled by a unit within the cataloging department. Except for the law, biomedical, and engineering and mathematical sciences libraries, the serials department provides centralized ordering and maintenance of payment records. Centralized receipt of subscriptions is achieved to a far lesser extent, with about half the branch libraries receiving subscriptions directly.

The serials department also operates the URL periodical reading room. Because of this aspect of the department's activities, some of its staff are involved in acquisitions decisions on periodical titles for URL. They review a variety of sources, looking for new periodical titles that may be appropriate for the URL collection. They frequently request sample issues of potential acquisitions and route them to appropriate materials selectors.

The collection-development officer in the University Library reports directly to the university librarian. This individual is responsible for coordinating the collection-development activities of all library units within the system and is the direct supervisor of twelve bibliographers. The bibliographers have the following geographical or subject-area responsibilities: Germanic, Slavic, Near Eastern, Indo-Pacific, Western European, Latin-American, African, Asian, Jewish Studies, social sciences, humanities, and medieval-Renaissance. These specialists select materials for only the University Research Library; hence their selections are, with few exceptions, titles appropriate to disciplines in the humanities and social sciences. Furthermore, in those disciplines covered by branch libraries, for example, art, music, education, and psychology, their selection activities tend to be limited.

The last unit to be discussed is the planning and systems department. This department is responsible for both automation activities and long-range planning. It also includes a task force. Among the libraries included in this study, the task force is a unique feature. The ten individuals in this group are assigned to work temporarily anywhere in the system where the need for more personnel becomes apparent. Thus, although formally with planning and systems, they can be assigned to work elsewhere in response to the needs of the larger system.

Primary responsibility for preparing the UCLA library budget rests with the assistant university librarian for planning and systems. Early in the fiscal year, the UCLA chancellor's office requests preliminary budgets from all major units on the campus. After consultation with the university librarian and relevant department heads throughout the library, the planning office prepares the first draft of a budget. The primary emphasis in the budget-making process is on increases or decreases of various funds relative to the prior year's budget. The budget is then submitted to the chancellor's office and reviewed by the assistant provost for planning. The budget is also submitted to a library planning office, which is a part of the systemwide administration for all campuses of the University of California. In this office, the budget is reviewed relative to the proposed budgets of all campus libraries. Changes and revisions in the budget may be made as a result of input, from either the UCLA administration or the library planning office.

The final budget for the University of California (UC) is prepared by the systemwide administration and submitted to the regents for their approval. Library allocations appear as ten line-items, one separate allocation for each campus library and a systemwide allocation. The budget approved by the regents is then transmitted to the governor for final submission to the state legislature.

In 1977, the library planning office began to phase in a method of budgeting for acquisitions in the UC libraries designed to ensure that universitywide acquisitions would attain a specific level for each unit in the system. Using a formula for assessing the acquisition level appropriate for the system, the office calculated that the funds available for the purchase of library materials were approximately 14 percent below what was needed. With this as a justification, the office attempted to increase the acquisitions portion of the UC library budget to compensate for the discrepancy between its present level and the level considered more adequate. Furthermore, the office intended to rely on the formula to distribute the total acquisitions budget for UC libraries among the nine campus libraries. These goals for acquisitions budgeting were to be phased in over four years, but, owing to the passing of Proposition 13 in 1978, there was a disruption in these plans. It is not yet clear what direction this systemwide planning effort will take.

Typically, the library is informed of its budget shortly after the beginning of the new fiscal year. For the past four or five years, in early fall, the library has received additional funds for acquisitions from the UCLA chancellor's discretionary funds. These additional monies have ranged from 7 to 10 percent of the state's allocation for acquisition.

In 1977-1978, UCLA library expenditures totaled almost $12 million. Salaries, wages, and personnel benefits accounted for 65 percent. Library materials, including binding, cost $3.1 million, or 26 percent of total expenditures. The remaining 9 percent was spent on operating expenses. Approximately 43 percent of the materials budget purchased serials subscriptions. These resources allowed the UCLA libraries to add just over 116,000 volumes and a net of 1,536 new serials titles to the collection.

The systemwide administration of the University of California has indicated that future collection development on each campus must move in the direction of an integrated enterprise. To this end, a new program called "shared purchases" has been initiated. With the approval of a committee composed of the collection-development officers from each of the nine campuses, shared purchases are made for more expensive items. The committee approves the purchases and decides which campus will receive and subsequently share the items. Shared purchases are funded with a 2 percent levy on the materials budget of each campus. In 1977-1978, $277,000 was available for shared purchases. In practice thus far, most shared-purchase items have been housed at either UC Berkeley or UCLA, reflecting a recognition of a geographical bipolarization in the integrated systemwide activities. Berkeley and UCLA are the centers of collection-development activity in the northern and southern regions of the state.

The focus at the University of California clearly is on developing a statewide library system that will be an interdependent, collective, and integrated enterprise. There is variable enthusiasm for this approach, for it runs counter to the tradition of the local self-sufficiency long cherished by many academic librarians. As an example of a large-scale resource-sharing project, the experience of the University of California's integrated collection-development program will be most informative for those interested in further expanding resource-sharing activities in academic libraries.

Summary

It is, of course, impossible to present a summary of all the information contained in these concise profiles. However, table 3-1 highlights selected comparable information about each institution to give the reader some sense of the great range and diversity included in this book. The institutions were established over a 200-year period ranging from 1764 at Brown University to 1971 at Stockton State College. Institution budgets range from $6.7 million to almost $438 million, and faculty size varies from 91 to 2,313. Enrollment figures vary from several thousand in the colleges to over 30,000 in three of the universities. The different academic programs emphasized in each institution are depicted in the varying patterns of bachelor's, master's, and doctoral degrees awarded.

Table 3-2 shows similar variations in the holdings and operations of the libraries. The number of professional librarians ranges from 7 at Earlham

Table 3-1
Institutional Summary Data, 1977-1978

	Earlham	Stockton	Brown	Penn State[a]	North Carolina[b]	Wisconsin[c]	UCLA
Founded	1847	1971	1764	1855	1795	1848	1919
Total Expenditures ($000)	6,760	11,087	68,306	263,251	173,946	363,280	437,900
Faculty	91	170	460	1,662	1,853	2,236	2,313
Undergraduate Enrollment	1,015	3,823	5,492	30,437	13,587	25,604	20,193
Graduate Enrollment	45	—	1,442	3,557	5,257	7,505	11,560
Degrees							
Bachelor's	199	777	1,178	7,545	2,835	4,424	4,446
Sciences	30%	23%	30%	38%	16%	34%	36%
Social sciences	37%	66%	25%	51%	62%	51%	40%
Humanities	27%	10%	36%	8%	18%	14%	20%
Other	6%	1%	9%	3%	4%	1%	4%
Master's	—	—	192	1,260	896	2,058	2,284
Sciences	—	—	30%	36%	13%	34%	31%
Social sciences	—	—	28%	54%	70%	54%	50%
Humanities	—	—	34%	9%	17%	11%	18%
Other	—	—	8%	1%	—	1%	1%
Doctoral	—	—	192	340	271	657	766
Sciences	—	—	60%	46%	34%	49%	68%
Social sciences	—	—	15%	46%	38%	34%	24%
Humanities	—	—	22%	8%	27%	17%	8%
Other	—	—	3%	—	1%	—	—

[a] All academic units at University Park only.
[b] All academic units at Chapel Hill except health sciences and law school.
[c] All academic units at Madison except medical school and law school.

Table 3-2
Library Summary Data, 1977-1978

	Earlham	Stockton	Brown	Penn State[a]	North Carolina[b]	Wisconsin[c]	UCLA
Professional Librarians	7	14	47	74	80	89	155
Collection Size (000)	240	94	1,530	1,500	2,000	2,800	3,900
Volumes Added (000)	7	10	39	48	88	109	116
Serials Titles	1,300	1,600	12,500	23,000	24,000	47,000	57,000
Serials Added	—	100	1,020	247	818	2,599	Net
Serials Dropped	—	—	17	511	316	813	1,536
Interlibrary Loans	—	273	1,592	16,687	12,284	73,994	53,577
Interlibrary Borrows	2,000	4,158	932	5,089	2,710	20,197	30,189
Budget ($000)	275	1,019	2,710	5,472	5,246	6,439	11,965
Personnel	51%	44%	60%	61%	59%	61%	65%
Materials	43%	39%	34%	29%	34%	29%	26%
Operating	6%	17%	6%	10%	7%	10%	9%

[a] All academic units at University Park.
[b] All academic units at Chapel Hill except health sciences and law school.
[c] All academic units at Madison except medical school and law school.

College to 155 at UCLA. Collection size varies from 94,000 at Stockton State College to almost 4 million at UCLA. The holdings-and-additions figures demonstrate the same ranges of variation.

Let us pause at this point, review what has been covered in the book thus far, and suggest what is covered in subsequent chapters. After a general discussion of the organization of academic libraries and the field methods employed in researching this book, we present brief profiles of each of the seven institutions studied. Tables 3-1 and 3-2 compare and contrast these institutions along a number of dimensions. Despite their great diversity, commonalities exist across these organizations, four of which are highlighted. First, all receive their financial and administrative support from and are accountable to their parent institutions. Second, although their internal characteristics and environments vary considerably, their goals are consistent: to acquire and provide access to information needed by both current and anticipated future users. Third, all are service organizations and therefore confront the common difficulty of devising measures of performance with criteria that can be expressed only imprecisely or qualitatively. Finally, each of the institutions continuously faces the problem of allocating finite resources among the different subunits of its organization. It is this commonality, finite resource allocation, which is the primary focus of the remainder of this book.

A further summary of what has been presented thus far and is presented in subsequent chapters is provided by the distinction between structure and function in organizations. An analogy may be helpful here. The structure of an organization is comparable to the anatomy of an organism. Anatomy is concerned with the bones, muscles, and ligaments of which the body consists. On the other hand, the discipline of physiology is concerned with bodily processes, that is, function. In order to understand the human body, it is necessary to study both anatomy and physiology; in order to understand organizations, it is necessary to study both structure and function. Thus far we have described the structure of academic libraries. In the next two chapters, we examine a most important aspect of the function, that is, the processes of resource allocation as they relate to collection development.

4 Fund Allocation and Expenditures

In order to achieve their goals, organizations allocate their finite resources to different activities and departments. Optimal resource allocation is a fundamental and recurring problem, involving both short- and long-range planning in the assignment of funds, materials, and personnel to specific tasks. Ideally, goals are stated in advance and then translated into specific tasks. Necessary facilities, materials, and personnel are obtained to further these tasks, and an appropriate division of labor is devised for all subunits within the organization. Products or services are then created and disseminated. The primary task of managers and supervisors is to ensure that the sum of the efforts of all individuals and groups results in overall goal accomplishment for the organization.

How organizations allocate resources is a question that has fascinated both managers and students of a wide variety of organizations. One common perspective is the traditional theory of the firm. This theory posits that organizations behave rationally to reduce costs and maximize gains, and therefore resources are allocated to enhance profits. The assumption of consistently rational behavior is questionable in all types of organizations. Nevertheless, the theory of the firm has been fruitfully applied in organizations that are product-oriented, where gains can be calculated in dollars. However, it has not been especially useful for analyzing resource allocation in service-oriented organizations such as libraries, where the end product is not easily measured in dollars or any other universal metric.

More recently, scholars have recognized that resource allocation in organizations can be fruitfully analyzed from psychological, sociological, and political perspectives.[1] Bower provides a particularly useful interdisciplinary approach to identifying and analyzing an organization's resource-allocation policies and practices.

Resource allocation is a broad concept encompassing all aspects of an organization's activities. Our concern with resource allocation in libraries centers on collection development, namely, how academic libraries distribute their resources in order to collect a multiplicity of materials and provide access and other related services to their user community of faculty and students. Drawing on the work of Bower, we addressed the following six questions:

1. What planning process is used by an academic library to analyze its environment and resources and subsequently select goals for collection development, defined in terms of present and future user needs?

2. What is the implementation process by which resources are distributed to achieve these goals?
3. How are the planning and implementation processes related?
4. What procedures are employed to assess the planning and implementation processes?
5. What problems characterize the management of these processes?
6. What improvements can be recommended that may be generalized to other libraries?[2]

These six questions supplied a framework for our field activities. They provided a means to analyze the two basic components of collection development—fund allocation and item selection. As was mentioned in chapter 1, fund allocation refers to those policies and procedures governing decisions to distribute money for materials among various units, which may include branch libraries, bibliographers, academic departments, research institutes, and library departments, such as reference and special collections. On the other hand, item selection refers to the policies and procedures governing decisions to spend allocated funds. This chapter reports on fund allocation, and chapter 5 reports on item selection. At the conclusion of chapter 5 we return to the above six questions.

In this chapter we first review available data on the fiscal environment of the academic-library community as they relate to collection development. This information will help the reader place institution-specific data in a broader context. We then turn to a description of the process of fund allocation in the seven participating libraries. The final section of the chapter presents information on their actual commitment of resources to various disciplines, reporting separately for the sciences, social sciences, and humanities.

Fiscal Environment of Collection Development

Table 4-1 presents aggregate data describing the growth in the nation's academic-library resources during the period 1967 to 1979. Total volume count has increased 76 percent, from 295 million in 1967 to 519 million in 1979. The libraries included in these counts are those of two- and four-year colleges and those of universities. During this period, the nation experienced a growth in their number, from 2,300 in 1967 to 3,122 in 1979.

As can be seen in the table, volumes added increased during the late 1960s, then leveled off in the early 1970s, and finally declined in the late 1970s. This occurred despite the fact that each year more academic libraries were contributing to added volume counts, and together their annual expenditures for materials, as displayed in the last column of table 4-1, were rising

Table 4-1
Growth in Academic-Library Resources and Expenditures on Materials

Year	Number of Libraries	Volumes[a] (Millions)	Volumes Added[a] (Millions)	Periodical Titles Received[b] (Millions)	Expenditures on Materials (Millions)
1967[c]	2,300	295	22	3.4	156
1968	2,430	305	25	2.5	188
1969	2,500	329	26	2.6	213
1970[c]	2,570	354	26	3.0	230
1971	2,600	380	25	3.6	247
1972[c]	2,625	405	25	3.9	260
1973	2,900	407	25	3.9	282
1974[c]	2,950	426	25	4.0	300
1975[c]	3,000	436	25	4.1	312
1976	3,000	468	23	4.5	337
1977[c]	3,000	490	23	4.6	350
1978[c]	3,061	504	23	4.7	398
1979[d]	3,122	519	22	4.8	447

Source: Adapted from *The Bowker Annual of Library and Book Trade Information*, 23d ed. (New York: Bowker, 1978), pp. 246-247.

[a]Includes volumes in the book stock and volumes in the periodical collections.
[b]For 1967 and 1968, the figures are for serials, including periodicals, annuals, proceedings, transactions, and so on. Figures for the remaining years include only periodicals.
[c]Data for these years are estimates.
[d]Preliminary data from the Survey of College and University Libraries, Fall 1979, conducted by The National Center for Education Statistics in the Department of Education.

steadily. Figure 4-1 graphically summarizes the growth and expenditure data presented in table 4-1. The top graph combines the number of volume additions and the number of periodical titles received. When this graph is compared to the graph of expenditures below it, it seems that since 1972 academic libraries have been spending more each year and actually acquiring less.

The expenditure data given in table 4-1 and plotted in the figure are expenditures for all library materials, including nonbook formats. Thus, part of the discrepancy between rising costs and declining growth, as depicted in the figure, may reflect increasing attention on the part of the academic-library community to nontraditional formats. But certainly the major factor in this discrepancy is inflation; in recent years, the rate of inflation of materials traditionally purchased by academic libraries has been far outstripping increases in materials budgets.

Table 4-2 summarizes the prices of three types of U.S. publications during the period 1967 to 1979. As can be seen, the prices of the mainstays of library acquisitions, monographs and periodicals, have soared. Indeed, the average price of periodicals has nearly quadrupled. Serials services, publications which are revised, cumulated, or indexed by means of updated

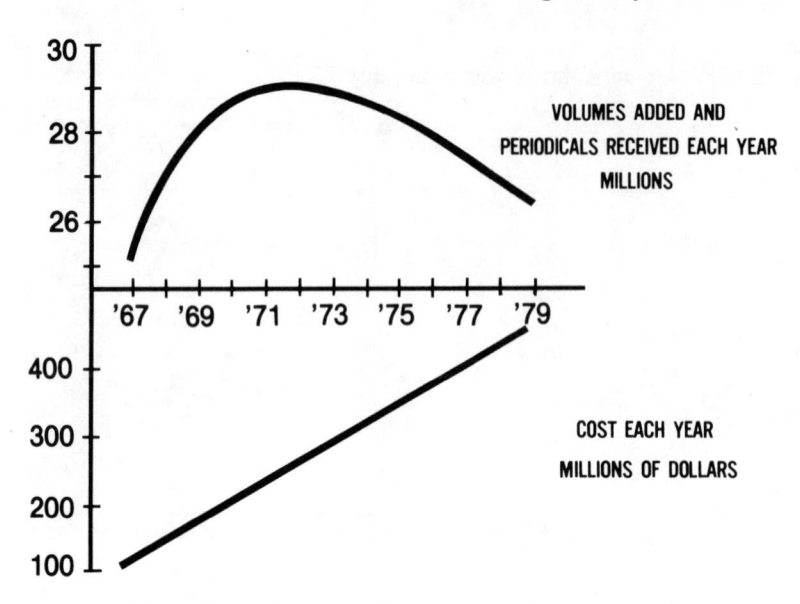

Figure 4-1. Academic Libraries' Acquisitions and Their Cost

Source: *The Bowker Annual of Library and Book Trade Information,* 23d ed. (New York: Bowker, 1978), pp. 246-247; preliminary data from the Survey of College and University Libraries, Fall 1979, conducted by the National Center for Education Statistics in the Department of Education.

or additional parts, have more than doubled in price. Although the rate of increase of all three formats has slowed considerably in the last few years, the average rate of each format has still exceeded the rate of increase in commitment of library resources to material purchases. Between 1975 and 1979 the annual increase in the amount libraries spend on materials averaged 8 percent. Over the last five years, the average annual increase in monographs has been 10 percent; periodicals, 11 percent; and serials services, 10 percent.[3]

Academic libraries tend to collect a great many foreign publications. Accurate data on the proportion of foreign acquisitions are not available, but in major university libraries it is not uncommon to find that at least 40 to 50 percent of the new acquisitions are published in foreign countries. Fry and White reported that between 1970 and 1976 foreign scholarly journals increased in price at an annual rate of 17.1 percent. Both the impact of inflation and the declining value of the dollar contribute to these escalating costs. Fry and White also report that those foreign journals more frequently ordered by academic libraries have increased in price even more rapidly than foreign scholarly journals in general, an annual rate of 18.1 percent from 1970 to 1976.[4]

Table 4-2
Increases in the Prices of U.S. Publications

Publication	1967-1969 Average Price ($)	1979 Average Price ($)	Percentage Increase
Monographs	8.77	22.80	160
Periodicals	8.66	30.37	251
Serial Services	72.42	171.06	136

Source: Adapted from *The Bowker Annual of Library and Trade Book Information*, 25th ed. (New York: Bowker, 1980), pp. 456-458.

Of course, the number of titles available each year has been steadily growing. In 1960, new monographs published in the United States numbered 15,000. By 1978, 41,000 new books were published, an increase of 175 percent.[5] For worldwide book production, it is estimated that an increase of 111 percent has occurred from 1955 to 1975.[6] Similarly, the number of serials published is expanding. King estimates that between 1960 and 1980 there will be a 44 percent increase in the number of U.S. journals published just for the sciences and social sciences.[7]

Thus, at least since 1972, the typical academic library has annually acquired a shrinking proportion of the market of new titles. This situation generates concern that libraries are becoming increasingly less able to satisfy the research and instructional needs of their users. Two more trends aggravate this problem.

First, funds for the operation of institutions of higher education are constrained. They have been through the 1970s, and all projections indicate such constraints will continue through at least the 1980s. In their struggle for their share of the funds, academic libraries are losing ground. Since 1972, total expenditures for academic libraries have risen 87 percent, from $796 million to $1,490 million; but the library portion of total college or university expenditures has been decreasing. Academic-library expenditures represented 4.8 percent of institutional expenditures in 1972 and only 3.7 percent in 1979.[8] The same pattern of the library's diminishing proportion of the college or university budget is also reported by Fry and White. Basing their conclusions on a sample of publicly supported institutions, Fry and White point out that while the college or university average budget increase was 10.4 percent per year, the average library budget increase was only 9.5 percent.[9]

The second trend reinforcing concern that libraries have lost and will continue losing ground in their collection development is the decreasing portion of total library expenditures on acquisitions. In 1967 acquisitions accounted for 40.8 percent of the money that academic libraries spent. This dropped to 34.9 percent in 1973 and still further in 1979 to 31.7 percent. It is interesting to note what library expenditures have gained those portions of the budget surrendered by acquisitions.

Figure 4-2 shows the major components of academic-library expenditures for 1967, 1973, and 1979. The figure demonstrates that personnel costs (that is, salaries, wages, and benefits) account for an increasing proportion of academic-library expenditures, rising from 53.4 percent in 1967 to 60.2 percent in 1979. In addition, operating expenses show an increase from 5.8 percent in 1967 to 7.7 percent in 1973 to 8.1 percent in 1979.

Fry and White indicate that between 1969 and 1973 academic libraries experienced a steady shift, averaging 0.5 percent per year, of funds from the materials to the salary budgets. Since 1974 this shift has been slowing down. In fact, Fry and White suggest that budgetary transfers from materials to labor budgets may cease while transfers from materials budgets to operating expenses become more dramatic.[10]

The fiscal plight of libraries over the last twelve years has had a differential impact on monographic as opposed to periodical acquisitions. The data of table 4-1 combine the counts of increasing numbers of academic libraries. Changes relevant to the typical academic library can be approximated by dividing a table datum by the number of libraries involved in the aggregate. Figure 4-3 summarizes the results of doing so for both volumes added and periodical titles received. The figure suggests that while the rate of volumes added has been declining, the number of periodical titles received by the typical library increased during the early 1970s and leveled off at the end of the decade.

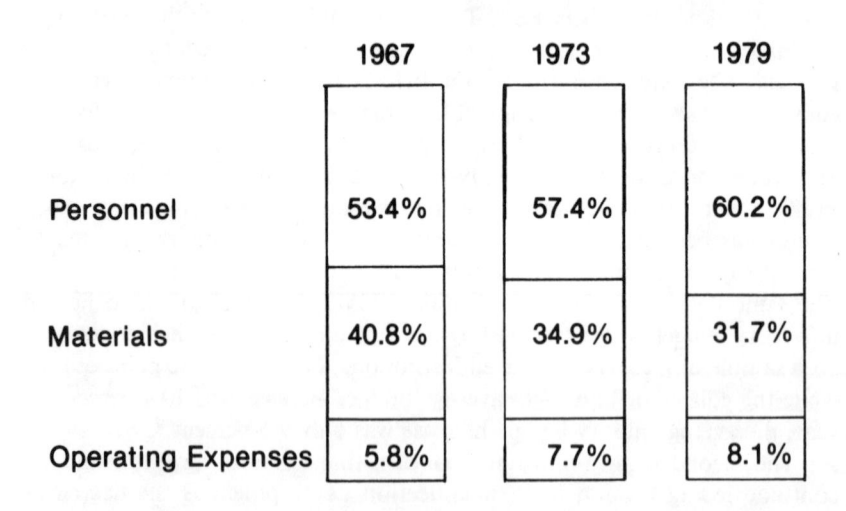

	1967	1973	1979
Personnel	53.4%	57.4%	60.2%
Materials	40.8%	34.9%	31.7%
Operating Expenses	5.8%	7.7%	8.1%

Source: *The Bowker Annual of Library and Book Trade Information*, 23d ed. (New York: Bowker, 1978), pp. 246-247; preliminary data from the Survey of College and University Libraries, Fall 1979, conducted by the National Center for Education Statistics in the Department of Education

Figure 4-2. Breakdown of Academic-Library Expenditures

Fund Allocation and Expenditures

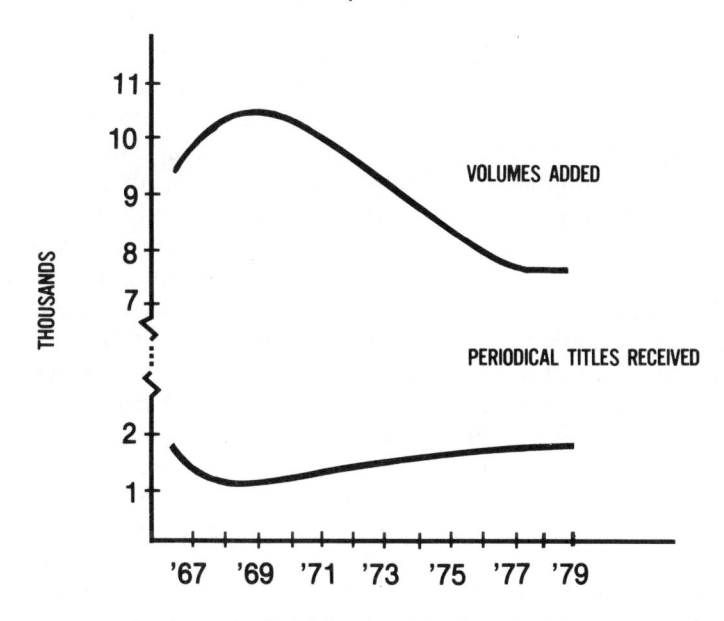

Source: *The Bowker Annual of Library and Book Trade Information*, 23d ed. (New York: Bowker, 1978), pp. 246-247; preliminary data from the Survey of College and University Libraries, Fall 1979, conducted by the National Center for Education Statistics in the Department of Education.

Figure 4-3. Typical Academic-Library Yearly Acquisition

Volumes added includes both books and bound periodicals. But if bound periodicals were removed from the top graph of figure 4-3, one would expect an even more dramatic drop in volumes added since periodical commitments have been increasing over the decade. Thus, the summary statement made earlier can be refined somewhat. It seems that, for at least the last few years, the typical academic library has been spending more each year and actually acquiring less, and what it has been acquiring less of is books.

In an earlier study, Fry and White also reported dramatic shifts in materials allocations from books to serials.[11] For larger academic libraries this shift was from $2.00 for monographs for every dollar spent on serials in 1969 to $1.16 in 1973. Their more recent data for 1973 to 1976 show clearly that this trend continued. By 1976 the large academic libraries were spending $0.77 on monographs for every dollar spent on serials.[12] Fry and White suggest that faculty members, particularly in the sciences and to a lesser extent in the social sciences, exert great pressure on library staff to expand serials collections. In these disciplines, book acquisitions are of lower priority.

Machlup and Leeson even more recently confirmed the Fry and White findings. They suggest academic libraries are devoting increasing shares of materials budgets to serials acquisitions and decreasing shares to book purchases. According to Machlup and Leeson, serials purchases increased from 34 percent of total acquisitions in 1970 to 50 percent in 1976, and the share of book purchases fell from 62 percent in 1970 to 44 percent in 1976.[13]

With continuing constraints on materials allocations, it is not surprising that response to budget pressures has centered on serials acquisitions. In their earlier study, Fry and White suggested that the common response to materials-budget pressures was to cancel duplicate subscriptions.[14] By 1978, they reported that libraries responded to continuing fiscal pressures by further canceling single subscriptions and severely limiting new subscriptions.[15] The former action suggests that libraries began to evaluate more critically their lists of subscriptions, and the latter action reflects the seriousness of the fiscal constraints. Again, the Machlup and Leeson survey confirmed the Fry and White data. The most frequently cited action taken by the libraries in their sample was the cancellation of single subscriptions. The next most frequent was the limiting of new titles added to subscription lists.[16]

In summary, growth in library collections and staff, and the services they support, has stagnated because of inflation. Although expenditures for books, salaries, and wages have been increasing, book stocks are increasing at declining rates; and staff size is actually decreasing.[17] Periodicals have been less affected by fiscal constraints as academic libraries have chosen to maintain and even add to their subscriptions. Of course, periodicals have not escaped the wrath of inflation. To maintain subscriptions, libraries have had to significantly increase periodical expenditures at the expense of increases in book expenditures.

As noted in chapter 2, the resources available for this investigation restricted our focus to the status of seven institutions in the spring of 1978. Since we could not obtain sufficient historical data on the materials expenditures of these seven libraries, we cannot adequately compare their experience over the past twelve years with that of academic libraries in general. Nevertheless, these trend data do provide a broad context within which to examine more detailed data on collection development in the comparative case studies.

Fund Allocation: An Overview

Figure 4-4 shows the stages which dollars must pass through before they are finally allocated for the purchase of library materials. The library budget is a segment of the academic institution's overall budget, and the materials budget is a portion of the total library budget. As was suggested in the pre-

Fund Allocation and Expenditures

INSTITUTIONAL BUDGET

⬇ — PRESIDENT, PROVOST / LIBRARY DIRECTOR

LIBRARY BUDGET

⬇ — LIBRARY DIRECTOR / SENIOR ADMINISTRATIVE STAFF

MATERIALS BUDGET

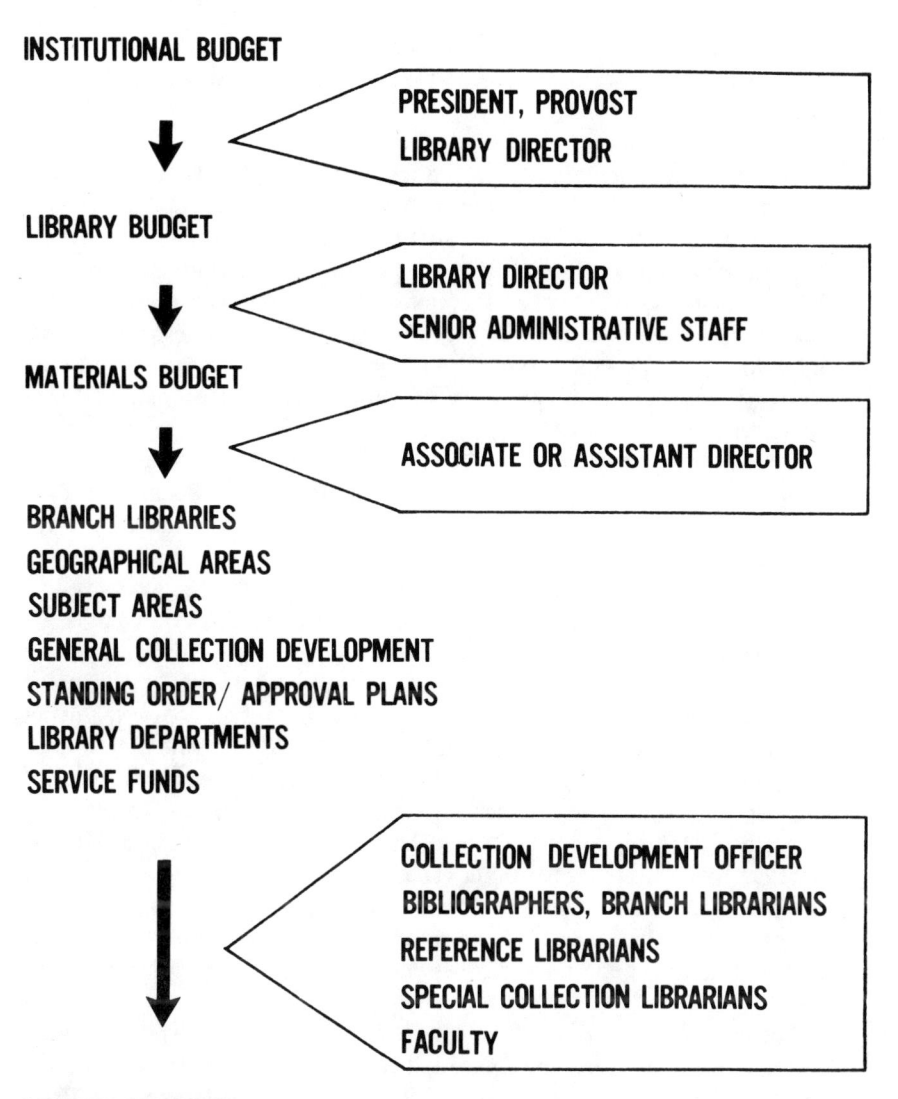

⬇ — ASSOCIATE OR ASSISTANT DIRECTOR

BRANCH LIBRARIES
GEOGRAPHICAL AREAS
SUBJECT AREAS
GENERAL COLLECTION DEVELOPMENT
STANDING ORDER/ APPROVAL PLANS
LIBRARY DEPARTMENTS
SERVICE FUNDS

⬇ — COLLECTION DEVELOPMENT OFFICER / BIBLIOGRAPHERS, BRANCH LIBRARIANS / REFERENCE LIBRARIANS / SPECIAL COLLECTION LIBRARIANS / FACULTY

LIBRARY MATERIALS

Figure 4-4. Resource Allocation: Principal Decision Makers

vious section, on the typical campus the library budget is about 4 percent of the institution's budget, and the materials budget is about 30 percent of the library's budget. Of course, a library may have other sources of money available for the purchase of materials: endowments, research grants, and other special funds. But for many academic libraries, and particularly public institutions, the main source of money for materials is the parent institution.

The principal actors in decisions concerning the allocation of each budget to the item or items below it appear on the right of the figure. The diagram oversimplifies the decision structure surrounding fund allocation. First, it can be argued that such a variety of organizations and practices exist among academic institutions that no single scheme is representative. Second, for almost all academic institutions, more individuals are involved in these processes than indicated by the diagram. But despite these limitations, for a typical campus figure 4-4 does suggest the levels of the institutional hierarchy most critically involved in the various stages of the fund-allocation process.

Considering the present fiscal state of libraries, one would expect much faculty awareness of and even involvement in the process of committing the materials budget to various areas of the collection, especially as the process pertains to materials purchased in support of their particular research and instructional interests. But on most campuses only a few faculty have any idea how money for materials is allocated or how their subject-area interests are faring relative to those of their colleagues.

Figure 4-4 lists the major units which are allocated dollars from the materials budget. Several of the terms describing these units need further elaboration. The fourth entry, general collection development, refers to money held by the library for discretionary or special purposes, such as the purchase of an expensive research collection. The term *library departments* refers to funds supporting foreign and domestic exchange programs, reference collections, and other specific collections (such as maps, documents, rare books, and the like). The last entry, service funds, refers to monies held by the library for the purchase of reserve materials, replacement copies, added copies, and other general maintenance and support activities.

For any given fund usually one individual is assigned the responsibility of spending the monies. The figure indicates the groups from which these fund administrators are drawn: the collection-development officer, bibliographers, branch librarians, reference librarians, special-collection librarians, and faculty. These fund administrators seldom reallocate their monies. They spend the funds they control as purchases come to their attention.

Among librarians and faculty, those who are designated fund administrators are also usually the principal item selectors. Other than those librarians and faculty given direct authority to spend an allocation, very few make any further contributions to general collection development or to specific item selection.

Patterns of Fund Allocation among Seven Academic Libraries

Having set a general context for fund allocation, we now turn to a microanalysis of fund-allocation policies and practices in seven academic libraries. In all institutions, we found a very striking common element in the fund-allocation procedures employed. During the course of our research, we asked 200 academic librarians how funds were allocated in their libraries. Invariably they reported that monies were allocated among various book funds in accordance with how funds had been distributed in previous years. The proportions may be adjusted slightly from year to year because the prices of materials in different subject areas have inflated at different rates, or a particular fund administrator complained more loudly than usual about the previous year's allocation. But in each institution there was a primary reliance on past allocations for the pattern of current allocations.

As students of a variety of complex organizations, we are compelled to comment on this uniformity of response. Middle- and upper-level managers in other organizations, for example, business corporations, would not indicate that their resource-allocation decisions depend so heavily on past practices. Indeed, in many organizations, there are sanctions against such overt and ritualistic observance of previous behaviors. Managers are typically encouraged to be innovative and, with an eye toward the future, produce new approaches and solutions rather than accept the past as a guide. Corporate executives who indicated that they did things in their units much the way things had been done the preceding year would probably not last very long in their positions. Of course, all organizations are compelled to repeat many types of behavior and frequently look to the immediate past for guidance. But it is certainly not the central ethos of management perspectives in most organizations. Regardless of how they actually behave, managers in most complex organizations would not readily verbalize their reliance on the past.

The academic librarians we interviewed accurately recognized that very little change occurs in the proportion of funds allocated to different library units from one year to the next. Exactly why past patterns are used to determine future patterns cannot be explained definitely, for clearly there are other options. The library literature offers many pertinent suggestions. Certainly one contributor to reliance on past distributions is the current fiscal environment within which libraries operate. In a period of fiscal constraint, any major modification in the pattern of allocation would necessitate cutbacks for some units. Because library units have so many continuing commitments, major cuts would seriously affect the amount of money available for discretionary spending and perhaps force termination of continuing commitments. Thus a major redirection of financial resources could result in chaos for some units. Furthermore, faculty served by the cut units might oppose the change in policy, creating a political situation which would further compound the problems of library management. Thus, if change is to be judiciously introduced in the pattern of fund allocation, often it is both administratively and politically expedient to proceed sequentially with only minor adjustments.

Although in each of the institutions similar patterns of expenditure are retained from year to year, the institutions do vary in the mechanics employed to arrive at these allocations. The libraries can be placed into three categories with respect to similarity of allocation procedures. The first group, including Earlham, Brown, Penn State, and UCLA, delegates responsibility for allocating funds to one individual. He or she locates the necessary data, such as current inflationary factors in different disciplines. These data are applied to last year's expenditures to arrive at new allocations. Before allocations are announced to fund administrators, the person responsible for assigning funds may consult with other library staff members, including the library director. In these institutions the proportions of the total budget given to each unit as well as absolute dollar amounts are not publicly announced. There is no elaborate effort to keep the figures secret; apparently there is little interest among either librarians or faculty in comparisons among specific allocations.

The second group of institutions includes Stockton and Wisconsin. In these institutions, funds are allocated according to a rather fixed set of percentages. In contrast with libraries in the first group, Stockton and Wisconsin publicly announce the percentages used to distribute the acquisitions budget. These percentages have remained constant for several years, and there is little expectation that they will be modified substantially in the near future. However, both Stockton and Wisconsin anticipate periodic reviews of the percentages; hence there is always some possibility of adjustments.

The third group includes one institution—North Carolina. At Chapel Hill, a library staff member is charged with drawing up a first draft of the allocations. The library administrative board, composed of both faculty and library staff, carefully reviews these recommendations. Modifications may result as part of the review process. Frequently testimony will be solicited from various individuals requesting additional funds. The board operates in a highly political context, and membership is perceived throughout the university as an important and prestigious assignment.

Expenditures by Format and Discipline

Allocations to funds reflect anticipated behavior. Expenditures describe actual behavior. Seldom does anticipated match actual behavior in a complex social structure, and the academic library is no exception. Typically some fund administrators will be lax in executing their item-selection responsibilities and not spend all allocated monies. Library staff may then claim these balances and encumber them for materials which have little substantive relation to the initial intent of the allocations. Frequently, the balances may be used to supplement the resources of a fund administrator who has energetically overspent his or her allocation. For many libraries, budgets do not remain stable throughout the year. Some may experience cutbacks which force modification of the original allocations. Others, particularly public institutions, may experience end-of-year windfalls which demand immediate altering of previously established priorities in order to encumber funds before the close of a fiscal year.

In this section we analyze the materials expenditures of each of the seven institutions for fiscal year (FY) 1977-1978. We concentrate on only expenditures directly related to material purchases and do not include personnel costs or binding. Also, we were unable to include materials obtained without cost, for example, gifts, exchange items, and documents. In many libraries, particularly large research libraries, these materials account for a substantial proportion of yearly acquisitions.

The data are presented by both the format of materials purchased and the scholarly disciplines served by the collections. In all institutions except Stockton, the format categories are monographs and serials. Expenditures on audiovisual materials, microforms, maps, and other special formats are merged into the book and serial categories, following the practices of each institution. Generally this means that the cost of any nonbook material acquired on a subscription basis is included within serials. All other expenditures on nonbook formats fall under monographs. For Stockton, three formats are distinguished: monographs, serials, and media. In 1977-1978, Stockton committed 7.5 percent of its materials budget to audiovisual material. In comparison, the audiovisual acquisitions of the other six institutions were minute.

As noted in chapter 1, the exact types of materials designated as serials vary from library to library. With one exception, the data presented for these seven libraries share a common definition. Generally what is considered a serial at one institution is considered a serial at another. But at Earlham College, only periodicals are designated serials. This is a less comprehensive definition than is employed at the other six libraries. However, since most subscriptions received by Earlham are periodicals, there is minimal risk of distortion in comparing the Earlham serials expenditures with those of the other institutions.

The second classification employed in this section is scholarly discipline. Monies made available in 1977-1978 to specific funds, that is, academic departments, library departments, undergraduate programs, research centers, professional schools, and graduate training programs, were placed in one of three major categories: sciences, social sciences, and humanities.

Figure 4-5 details the placement of these funds. Entries in the table are not exhaustive of all academic departments and programs in U.S. colleges and universities. Rather, they are a listing of book funds designated in the materials allocations of the seven institutions. One might engage in endless debates concerning such classification schemes. For example, history is placed in the humanities rather than the social sciences. The reader is invited to assess the appropriateness of our assignments.

Figure 4-5 includes two additional categories which are used in presenting the data of this section. The first, social science and humanities, includes funds available for the purchase of titles of relevance to either of these disciplines. Examples are funds supporting research and instruction in area studies, for example, Latin America or Western Europe. The second category, unclassifiable, includes funds for library services available to all disciplines (for example, replacements, reserves), funds supporting general collections (for example, reference), and funds based on format as opposed to discipline (for example, documents, maps, microforms). Many of the funds entered under social sciences and humanities and unclassifiable could have been distributed among the sciences, social sciences, and humanities categories, but it would have required a title-by-title sorting, a task beyond the resources available to us.

It should be pointed out that a number of problems were encountered in analyzing the financial resources committed to acquisitions. First, the assignment of funds to different categories frequently did not correspond to the financial record-keeping practices of the institutions. For example, in some institutions history was considered a social science. We have reorganized all data to fit a scheme consistent with figure 4-5. Second, at UCLA, 1977-1978 resource commitments could not be distributed between monographs and serials, for they are not initially so designated. Therefore,

SCIENCES	SOCIAL SCIENCES	HUMANITIES	SOCIAL SCIENCES & HUMANITIES
AGRICULTURE	ANTHROPOLOGY	ARCHITECTURE	AMERICAN CIVILIZATION
BIOLOGY	BUSINESS ADMINISTRATION	ART	AREA STUDIES
BOTANY	ECONOMICS	CLASSICS	FOLKLORE
CHEMISTRY	EDUCATION	ENGLISH	MINORITY STUDIES
ENGINEERING	GEOGRAPHY	HISTORY	PEACE STUDIES
GEOLOGY	JOURNALISM	HISTORY OF SCIENCE	UNDERGRADUATE LIBRARY
HEALTH SCIENCES	LAW	LANGUAGES	
MATHEMATICS	LIBRARY SCIENCE	LITERATURE	
PHARMACY	LINGUISTICS	MUSIC	UNCLASSIFIABLE
PHYSICS	MILITARY SCIENCE	PHILOSOPHY	
ZOOLOGY	PHYSICAL EDUCATION	RELIGION	EXCHANGE
	POLITICAL SCIENCE	SPEECH	GENERAL BIBLIOGRAPHY
	PSYCHOLOGY	THEATER ARTS	GENERAL REFERENCE
	PUBLIC ADMINISTRATION		GENERAL SERIALS
	RECREATION		GENERAL VENDOR CONTRACTS
	SOCIAL WORK		GOVERNMENT DOCUMENTS
	SOCIOLOGY		MAPS
	URBAN STUDIES		MICROFORMS
			PRESERVATION
			REPLACEMENTS

Figure 4-5. Discipline Groupings

1976-1977 expenditure data, which were available by format and Library of Congress (LC) classifications, were used. Finally, at Brown University, a general serials fund supports all serials taken by the library for at least three years. Only 1976-1977 data were available describing the discipline breakdown of the fund; these data were based on LC classifications. An extrapolation of the 1976-1977 breakdown to 1977-1978 serials expenditures is what is presented for Brown in table 4-5.

Table 4-3 shows the distribution of expenditures for Earlham College in 1977-1978. The bottom line displays a typical college-expenditure pattern across formats. More is spent for the purchase of monographs than for serials, with 65.1 percent of the total buying books. This pattern was also observed at Stockton State College and at the undergraduate libraries in the universities included in this study. Serial titles are often specialized research materials, beyond the scope of a college collection.

The distribution of total expenditures by discipline reflects an acquisitions emphasis on the natural sciences and humanities, each receiving roughly equal shares of the total materials budget, 25.5 and 29.2 percent, respectively. In contrast, the social sciences receive 14.9 percent. The sciences account for the largest proportion of the serials budget, 39.1 percent, and the humanities account for the largest portion of the monograph budget, 36.4 percent.

In table 3-1, we pointed out that Earlham College granted more degrees in the social sciences (37 percent) than in either the sciences (30 percent) or the humanities (27 percent). Yet table 4-3 indicates that only 15 percent of total expenditures were for the social sciences. Undoubtedly, some portion of the 30 percent of unclassifiable materials is used to support the social sciences, but the pattern of underbuying for the social sciences relative to

Table 4-3
Distribution of Materials Expenditures by Format and Discipline Categories, Earlham College, 1977-1978
(percent)

Discipline	Monographs	Serials	Total
Sciences	18.2	39.1	25.5
Social Sciences	13.4	17.7	14.9
Humanities	36.4	15.6	29.2
Unclassifiable	32.0	27.6	30.4
Total	100.0	100.0	100.0
	($72,000)	($38,000)	($110,000)
Percentage of Total Materials Budget	65.1	34.9	100.0

the proportion of degrees awarded is common in many academic libraries. In comparison to the sciences and humanities, students in the social sciences, particularly at the undergraduate level, traditionally do not use library materials as extensively as their counterparts in other fields. It may well be that social-science courses tend to rely more heavily on textbooks, and courses in the humanities and the sciences involve greater use of materials more often included in the library's collection. This pattern of relative underspending for the social sciences is repeated in other libraries included in this study.

Table 4-4 shows the distribution of expenditures for Stockton State College. Again, the bottom line summarizes the library's overall commitment to the various formats: monographs, 57.4 percent; serials, 35.1 percent; and audiovisual materials, 7.5 percent. As at Earlham, the sciences command considerably more of the serials budget than do either the social sciences or the humanities. But in contrast to Earlham, there is relatively little difference among the sciences, social sciences, and humanities in their expenditures on monographs. This reflects a basic distinction between the two colleges. Earlham provides a more traditional, liberal-arts curriculum. Stockton's emphasis is more career-oriented.

Professional studies at Stockton comprise programs in business administration, the health professions, and information science. Expenditure data by program were not available. Hence, division expenditures could not be distributed among the sciences, social sciences, and humanities categories. In fact, except for some minor adjustments to make categories consistent with the discipline groupings of figure 4-5, the four discipline areas of table 4-4 correspond to the four major academic divisions of the college.

Table 4-4
Distribution of Materials Expenditures by Format and Discipline Categories, Stockton State College, 1977-1978
(percent)

Discipline	Monographs	Serials	Audiovisual	Total
Sciences	16.9	37.4	18.9	24.2
Social Sciences	18.5	16.1	19.1	17.7
Humanities	20.3	11.7	19.3	17.2
Professional Studies	10.5	14.5	22.5	12.8
Unclassifiable	33.8	20.3	20.2	28.1
Total	100.0	100.0	100.0	100.0
	($155,000)	($95,000)	($20,000)	($270,000)
Percentage of Total Materials Budget	57.4	35.1	7.5	100.0

For both monographs and media, Stockton allocates equal amounts of money to its four academic divisions. The variance in the percentages noted in the table reflects the fact that some divisions overspend and others underspend their allocations. In particular, the purchase of monographs in support of professional studies lagged far behind the monograph purchases in other areas.

During FY 1977-1978, Stockton spent an additional $55,000 on periodicals in microform, an expenditure not included in table 4-4. Relative to Stockton's expenditure of $270,000 for all other materials, this commitment to microforms is rather extraordinary. It reflects the fact that Stockton is a new library attempting to complete its basic collection. But there is another factor operating also. For the most part, Stockton retains in hard copy only current periodical issues. To conserve space and save binding costs, Stockton retains most back issues of periodicals on microform only. In fact, Stockton's binding costs in 1977-1978 were only $5,000, as compared to $7,400 at Earlham, an institution spending well under half of what Stockton spends for materials. It should also be pointed out that during 1977-1978 additional reference materials, costing almost $27,000, were added to Stockton's reference collection. This expenditure was entered in the unclassifiable category, accounting for nearly 36 percent of this category.

Brown expenditures appear in table 4-5. Here we note a pattern of expenditure by format that is more common in universities: almost 60 percent of the total materials budget is used for serials. The distribution among the scholarly disciplines shows a relatively heavy emphasis on sciences, accounting for nearly 42 percent of the total materials budget; and only 8 percent

Table 4-5
Distribution of Materials Expenditures by Format and Discipline Categories, Brown University, 1977-1978
(percent)

Discipline	Monographs	Serials	Total
Sciences	16.3	60.0	41.7
Social Sciences	7.0	7.9	7.5
Humanities	40.3	12.9	24.4
Social Sciences and Humanities	19.4	4.9	11.0
Unclassifiable	17.0	14.3	15.4
Total	100.0	100.0	100.0
	($325,000)	($449,000)	($774,000)
Percentage of Total Materials Budget	42.0	58.0	100.0

is expended for the social sciences—a pattern similar to that noted at Earlham. As mentioned in the Brown profile in chapter 3, social-science programs account for a substantial proportion of both the undergraduate and graduate degrees awarded. Again, had we been able to account for the social-science components of the social sciences and humanities and unclassifiable categories, this figure would have been higher. For example, documents heavily support the social-science curriculum at Brown, but because of the difficulty of analyzing the expenditure of almost $17,500 for documents, the entire fund was placed in the unclassifiable category.

Nevertheless, the Brown social-sciences figure is substantially lower than that of the other institutions included in this study. Contributing to this are the following factors. First, Brown does not offer Ph.D. programs in either education or political science. Second, through its participation in a Rhode Island consortium of libraries, Brown has access to some expensive social-science materials, for example, the Educational Resources Information Center (ERIC) and the Human-Relations-Area File. Finally, the substantive focuses of many research and instructional programs in the social sciences at Brown do not require extensive use of library resources. Rather, they tend to use computer programs and numerical data sets which traditionally have not been housed in libraries. It may be that the low figure for social sciences at Brown is partially explained by the librarians' acute sensitivity to their environment, fostered by an awareness of fiscal constraints. If social scientists as a rule infrequently use library materials, there is less need to assign them scarce library resources.

At Brown there is a strong predominance of serials acquisitions for the sciences, 60 percent, and monographic acquisitions for the humanities, 40.3 percent. Brown maintains a standing-order plan for university-press publications. Monographs arriving through the plan are primarily social-science and humanities titles. Thus, this expenditure was included among the social-science and humanities expenditures. In 1977-1978, the plan cost $22,200, or about 2.9 percent of total expenditures at Brown on materials.

As at Brown, the cost of serials at Penn State accounted for more than half of the library's materials expenditures. About 53 percent of the budget bought serials, as can be seen in table 4-6. Also as at Brown, the sciences consumed about 40 percent of the total budget. In contrast to Brown, purchases in support of the social sciences accounted for a greater share of the total budget, about 13.6 percent, while those in support of the humanities received a smaller share, 19.3 percent. Nevertheless, at Penn State, in comparison to the distribution of degrees awarded, the social sciences receive a relatively smaller portion of materials expenditures; and the humanities receive a larger portion.

Penn State frequently receives windfalls as the fiscal year draws to a close, and 1977-1978 was no exception. At the beginning of the year, the

Fund Allocation and Expenditures

Table 4-6
Distribution of Materials Expenditures by Format and Discipline Categories, The Pennsylvania State University, 1977-1978
(percent)

Discipline	Monographs	Serials	Total
Sciences	23.0	53.2	39.1
Social Sciences	20.6	7.4	13.6
Humanities	34.5	6.1	19.3
Social Sciences and Humanities	9.5	10.4	10.0
Unclassifiable	12.4	22.9	18.0
Total	100.0	100.0	100.0
	($655,000)	($751,000)	($1,406,000)
Percentage of Total Materials Budget	46.6	53.4	100.0

library anticipated a budget of about $1.2 million, 61 percent of which was allocated to support continuing subscriptions, leaving 39 percent for the purchase of books. Before the close of the year, additional resources totaling about $200,000 were routed into nonsubscription purchases.

The perennial problem the library faces with these windfalls is how to expend them effectively, before the fiscal year expires. Selectors have difficulty spending windfall monies on titles which they previously passed over with their smaller initial allocations; the acquisitions department cannot handle the resulting volume of work before the year runs out. Thus, in lieu of purchasing titles that may be considered essential by selectors for the collections for which they are responsible, the library tends to purchase expensive titles or sets that may be perceived as less essential, but necessary if all funds are to be spent in time.

As shown on table 4-7, North Carolina is not as heavily committed to serials subscriptions as Brown and Penn State. Only 40 percent of the materials budget is spent on serials. The remaining 60 percent supports monograph acquisitions. This concentration of materials funds on monographs reflects a number of factors: (1) the exclusion of the medical and health sciences from the Academic Affairs Library; (2) the absence of engineering, agriculture, and mineral sciences from the Chapel Hill campus; and (3) North Carolina's traditional emphasis on the humanities. For many years, the humanities have been very strong at Chapel Hill, and now they account for 30.8 percent of the materials budget. However, again we see the pattern observed at other institutions concerning the social sciences—large student enrollments, yet a small portion of materials expenditures.

Wisconsin's expenditure distribution, as displayed in table 4-8, is

Table 4-7
Distribution of Materials Expenditures by Format and Discipline Categories, The University of North Carolina, Chapel Hill, 1977-1978
(percent)

Discipline	Monographs	Serials	Total
Sciences	7.4	42.2	21.3
Social Sciences	17.9	14.7	16.6
Humanities	40.7	16.0	30.8
Social Sciences and Humanities	10.6	17.7	13.4
Unclassifiable	23.4	9.4	17.9
Total	100.0	100.0	100.0
	($787,000)	($524,000)	($1,311,000)
Percentage of Total Materials Budget	60.0	40.0	100.0

similar to that observed at Penn State. At Wisconsin, serials account for 53.7 percent of the expenditures. As a land-grant institution, Wisconsin has traditionally emphasized the sciences, which account for almost 40 percent of the total materials expenditures. As mentioned above, Wisconsin's medical library has not been included in our analysis of the campus' library resources. Had it been, the relative commitment of resources to the sciences would have been even greater.

About 21 percent of Wisconsin's expenditures were entered in the social sciences and humanities category. These were primarily funds spent by area bibliographers. Both North Carolina and UCLA also have substantial com-

Table 4-8
Distribution of Materials Expenditures by Format and Discipline Categories, University of Wisconsin, Madison, 1977-1978
(percent)

Discipline	Monographs	Serials	Total
Sciences	21.1	54.1	38.8
Social Sciences	18.9	15.5	17.1
Humanities	25.2	8.8	16.4
Social Sciences and Humanities	25.7	17.1	21.1
Unclassifiable	9.1	4.5	6.6
Total	100.0	100.0	100.0
	($775,000)	($900,000)	($1,675,000)
Percentage of Total Materials Budget	46.3	53.7	100.0

Fund Allocation and Expenditures

mitments to area programs, but for both sites we were able to distribute these commitments between humanities and social sciences. Hence, for both North Carolina and UCLA, area program expenditures do not appear in the combined category.

As mentioned in the beginning of this chapter, expenditure data for the University of California, Los Angeles, is for FY 1976-1977. Table 4-9 portrays the distribution. Like UNC Chapel Hill, UCLA commits more than half of its resources to monograph acquisitions; these accounted for 56.7 percent of the 1976-1977 expenditures. One might expect that a larger portion of the materials budget expended on monographs is characteristic of an institution whose strongest academic programs are in the humanities, but the distribution of total resources does not suggest an academic program emphasis on the humanities. In fact, resource commitments to the sciences, social sciences, and humanities are almost identical—32.3, 29.1 and 29.5 percent, respectively. Looking within serials and monographs, we find a pattern consistent with that of the other institutions. The sciences account for the largest portion of serials expenditures, 46.8 percent, and the humanities account for the largest portion of the monograph expenditures, 38.6 percent.

In order to summarize the expenditure data presented for each institution, we have prepared table 4-10, which reports on serials expenditures for each dollar spent on monographs. These data are displayed separately by institution and, within each institution, by groupings of scholarly disciplines. Because this table is different from those presented earlier, an explanation of its contents is given. Looking at the first row, one should interpret the data as follows: At Earlham College, for each dollar spent on monographs in the sciences, $1.15 was spent on serials. Correspondingly, for each dollar

Table 4-9
Distribution of Materials Expenditures by Format and Discipline Categories, University of California, Los Angeles, 1976-1977
(percent)

Discipline	Monographs	Serials	Total
Sciences	21.3	46.8	32.3
Social Sciences	33.3	23.6	29.1
Humanities	38.6	20.1	30.6
Social Sciences and Humanities	6.9	1.6	4.6
Unclassifiable	0.0	7.9	3.4
Total	100.0	100.0	100.0
	($1,627,000)	($1,240,000)	($2,867,000)
Percentage of Total Materials Budget	56.7	43.3	100.0

Table 4-10
Serials Commitment for Each Dollar Spent on Monographs
(dollars)

Institution	Sciences	Social Sciences	Humanities	Social Sciences and Humanities	Total
Earlham College	1.15	0.71	0.23	—	0.54
Stockton State College	1.36	0.53	0.35	—	0.61
Brown University	5.08	1.58	0.44	0.35	1.38
The Pennsylvania State University	2.65	0.41	0.20	1.26	1.15
University of North Carolina, Chapel Hill	3.81	0.55	0.26	1.11	0.67
University of Wisconsin, Madison	2.98	0.95	0.40	0.77	1.16
University of California, Los Angeles	1.67	0.54	0.40	0.18	0.76

spent on monographs in the social sciences, $0.71 was spent on serials; and for each dollar spent on monographs in the humanities, $0.23 went for serials. In all disciplines combined at Earlham, for each dollar spent on monographs, $0.54 went for serials.

Reading down the right-hand column of the table, we note that the lowest rate of serials expenditures relative to monographs is the $0.54 at Earlham College. Correspondingly, Brown spent $1.38 on serials for each monograph dollar and therefore had the highest rate of acquisition of serials relative to monographs.

Looking down the sciences column, we note that more money is spent for serials than for monographs in all institutions. But this is particularly the case in the universities and more exceptionally the case at Brown University. As mentioned above, Brown's collection strengths are in the humanities and the sciences, with the sciences commanding over 40 percent of the total acquisitions budget. The expenditure of over $5 on serials in the sciences for each dollar spent on monographs dramatically illustrates the influence of both the dependence on serials as opposed to monographs in the sciences and Brown's program emphasis on the sciences.

With the exception of Brown, the social sciences at all institutions studied spend more money on monographs than serials. In this respect, Brown is again an informative case. Although it may appear as though the social sciences commit a significant portion of their money to serials, it may be more accurate to say that the social sciences are allocated little money; hence, to maintain a basic serials collection, a significant portion of their money must be commited to serials.

The humanities column shows clearly that in all institutions there is a much heavier reliance on monographic materials than on serials. The types of funds included in the social sciences and humanities category varied considerably more across the universities than did those entered in the other discipline clusters. This variety is reflected in the figures presented in the fourth column.

The expenditure data can be further summarized by using the two dimensions of discipline and format. Of the institutions included in this study, none emphasizes the social sciences in its commitment of resources. Either the sciences or the humanities are emphasized by four institutions—Brown, Penn State, Wisconsin, and North Carolina. The sciences are stressed at Brown with a 42 percent commitment, at Penn State University with 39 percent, and at the University of Wisconsin with 39 percent. These patterns clearly reflect the substantive training programs which have traditionally been strongest on these three campuses. Brown University's emphasis reflects both its tradition in the natural sciences and mathematics and its recently established medical program. Penn State and Wisconsin have substantial agriculture, engineering, and mineral-science programs.

At North Carolina the humanities receive the largest allocation, 31 percent. Although it is a land-grant institution, North Carolina does not stress those science programs that are usually part of land-grant institutions. Again we remind the reader that the Health Sciences Library at North Carolina has not been included within the purview of this study, because it is an independent library reporting to the dean of the medical school. Had the health-science allocation been included, the humanities might not appear the predominant recipient of materials resources at Chapel Hill.

The two colleges, Earlham and Stockton, and UCLA do not emphasize one of the discipline groupings to the same extent as the other four institutions. Particularly interesting is UCLA, for it demonstrates the pattern of a university library which supports such a variety of academic programs that almost identical allocations are assigned to each grouping of disciplines.

The second dimension on which these data can be summarized is the format of materials, that is, monographs in comparison to serials. Here the seven institutions show substantial variability in the proportion of resources allocated to serials, ranging from 35 percent at the two colleges, Earlham and Stockton, to 58 percent at Brown. Among the universities, the University of North Carolina assigns least to serials, 40 percent. With a 43 percent commitment, UCLA is quite similar. The other universities have much higher commitments—Brown University, 58 percent; Penn State, 53 percent; the University of Wisconsin, 54 percent. It is interesting to speculate on possible causes of these differences among institutions in the proportion of resources allocated to serials.

The use of a general serials fund to support subscriptions is a common phenomenon in academic libraries. Under such a system, the cost of a subscription is covered at some point by a general fund. Funds allocated to faculty and library staff are used primarily to acquire new subscriptions and books; continuing commitments become the responsibility of the general fund. Brown University, Penn State, and Wisconsin maintain general serials funds. Such a general serials fund is not used at UCLA, where the cost of continuing commitments initiated by a fund is maintained as the responsibility of that fund. The administrator responsible for the fund decides on how much of the allocation will be expended on monographs, continuing serials, and new serials. North Carolina, with the lowest serials subscription rate, only recently has initiated a general serials fund. It may be the case that requiring individual funds to bear the cost of the subscriptions they initiate impedes the expansion of serials and a corresponding diminution of the monograph budget. However, a decentralized system for serials acquisition runs the risk of unnecessary duplication and gaps, particularly in serials that are relevant to interdisciplinary programs. The serials committee of the library administrative board at North Carolina is given specific responsibility and authority to monitor such problems.

One final comment before we conclude our discussion of expenditures. In this section expenditures were analyzed, focusing on those monies which are allocated to buy books, serials, and other formats. We did not analyze the indirect costs of collection development, the foremost being the personnel resources committed to the process. Unfortunately, we did not have the resources to pursue this question. But the comparison of tables 4-3 through 4-9 with similar tables distributing personnel costs would be most interesting.

At this point, however, it is possible to speculate what such analyses would reveal by considering the kinds of personnel involved in item selection in the various disciplines. In university libraries science fund administrators tend to be heads of branch libraries, but social science and humanities selectors tend to be bibliographers. The latter are usually more senior personnel and frequently have graduate degrees in their subject specialties. Although we cannot verify it with empirical data, we strongly suspect that the average salary of bibliographers exceeds the average salary of branch librarians. Therefore, we would anticipate that in those university libraries with substantial staffs of bibliographers, an analysis of the personnel cost of collection development might reveal that a larger portion of the library's overall resources is invested in collection development in the humanities and the social sciences than in the sciences.

Rather than present a summary of the material discussed in this chapter, we now turn to the policies and procedures governing item selection in the seven academic libraries. Following the discussion of this material we present a summary of chapters 4 and 5.

Notes

1. See, for example, Kenneth Arrow, *Social Choice and Individual Values*, Cowles Commission Monograph 12. (New York: John Wiley & Sons, 1951); Herbert Simon, *Models of Man*. (New York: 1957); and Joseph L. Bower, *Managing the Resource Allocation Process: A Study of Corporate Planning and Investment* (Boston: Graduate School of Business Administration, Harvard University, 1970).

2. Bower, ibid., p. 24.

3. *The Bowker Annual of Library and Book Trade Information*, 25th ed. (New York: Bowker, 1980), p. 456-458.

4. Bernard M. Fry and Herbert S. White, "Impact of Economic Pressures on American Libraries and Their Decisions Concerning Scholarly and Research Journal Acquisitions and Retention," final report to the Division of Science Information, U.S. National Science Foundation, Grant no. DSI 76-23592, Graduate Library School, Indiana University, Bloomington, June 1978, pp. 147-150.

5. *Statistical Abstract of the United States 1979* (Washington: Government Printing Office, 1979), p. 593.

6. *Statistical Yearbook, 1976* (Paris: UNESCO, 1977), p. 802.

7. D.W. King, *Statistical Indicators of Scientific and Technical Communication, 1960-1980* (Washington: National Science Foundation, 1976), Contract NSF C-878, p. 31.

8. *The Bowker Annual*, 1978, p. 247; and preliminary data from the Survey of College and University Libraries, Fall 1979, conducted by the National Center for Education Statistics in the Department of Education.

9. Fry and White, "Impact of Economic Pressures on American Libraries," p. 10.

10. Ibid., p. 10.

11. Bernard M. Fry and Herbert S. White, *Publishers and Libraries: The Study of Scholarly and Research Journals* (Lexington, Mass.: LexingtonBooks, D.C. Heath and Company, 1976), pp. 47-49.

12. Fry and White, "Impact of Economic Pressures on American Libraries," pp. 11-12.

13. Fritz Machlup and Kenneth Leeson, *Information through the Printed Word: The Dissemination of Scholarly, Scientific, and Intellectual Knowledge*, vol. 3: *Libraries* (New York: Praeger Publishers, 1978), pp. 61-64.

14. Fry and White, *Publishers and Libraries*, pp. 47-49.

15. Fry and White, "Impact of Economic Pressures on American Libraries," pp. 90-92.

16. Machlup and Leeson, *Information through the Printed Word*, vol. 3, pp. 70-72.

17. Theodore Samore, "College and University Library Statistics: Analysis of NCES Survey," in *The Bowker Annual of Library and Book Trade Information*, 23d ed. (New York: Bowker, 1978), p. 243.

5 Item Selection

In this chapter we discuss item selection, the second aspect of collection development. As defined in chapter 1, item selection is the process of identifying and designating new materials for addition to the collection. First, we provide an overview of the principal actors involved in this process: library staff, faculty members, and commercial vendors. This discussion includes a description of their principal collection-development activities and their patterns of communication. We follow this discussion with a description of item selection in each institution. Emphasis is placed on commonly used identification tools and the relative contributions of different categories of individuals to the collection-development process.

The chapter then reviews item-selection procedures in six disciplines, focusing on patterns across rather than within institutions. A number of different issues are raised, including collection development in branch libraries for the sciences, the role of bibliographers in selecting for the humanities and social sciences, and the use of blanket-order or approval plans to facilitate the development of a library's collections. The analysis then returns to the six questions raised at the beginning of chapter 4. Throughout the chapter, problems in the organization of collection development in academic libraries are highlighted.

General Overview

The authority to spend acquisition funds is distributed among three groups: library staff, faculty members, and commercial vendors. The vendors referred to here are those under contract to the library to select and supply titles. They may be publishers or jobbers, the distributors of the products of publishers. Although vendors are not formally designated as administrators of library funds, they participate in item selection in much the same way as librarians and faculty. Libraries employ them to build prespecified areas of the collection or supply all titles produced by a selected list of publishers.

The portion of the total acquisitions budget assigned to library staff, faculty members, or vendors determines the relative impact of these groups on overall collection development. The distribution of authority to spend materials funds critically influences which titles are acquired for the library, for it determines the constellation of persons involved in item selection.

For example, faculty tend to become more active participants in item selection when portions of the materials budget are earmarked for their control.

The acquisitions budget has two components: money to support continuing subscriptions maintained by the library and money uncommitted to such continuing obligations and thus free to be used for the purchase of books, new subscriptions, or other materials, that is, microforms, audiovisuals, and so on. This uncommitted portion is distributed among a number of accounts, commonly called "book funds." As described in chapter 4, these funds are established for academic departments, research institutes, interdisciplinary programs, branch libraries, departments within the central library, or general library services, such as a fund for the purchase of replacements for lost copies. Funds may also be designated for vendor-selected materials. Usually only one person is formally authorized to approve the expenditure of a fund, although a number of persons may participate in deciding which materials are to be purchased. Faculty often administer funds associated with departmental or research-institute programs, and librarians administer funds for branch libraries, departments within the central library, and general services. Typically, funds associated with vendor contracts are monitored by bibliographers or librarians in the acquisitions department.

Figure 5-1 portrays communication links among the three groups involved in item selection and the acquisitions department. In the figure, acquisitions is included because of its special role in collection development. Seldom do members of the acquisitions department select items for purchase; their role is usually limited to acquiring titles after the decision to purchase has been made by faculty or other library staff members. This role is emphasized in the figure by the use of unidirectional arrows. Acquisitions librarians do initiate interactions with vendors, selectors within the library, and selectors among the faculty; but typically these communications pertain to selection decisions which have already been made.

For the most part, commercial vendors offering contractual arrangements restrict their communications to library staff, since the library is usually the agent responsible for negotiating such arrangements. The specification of what should be sent is most often prescribed by the collection-development officer, bibliographers, or branch librarians. If a faculty group desires a vendor's services, it typically requests that the library initiate the contract, for faculty rarely enter into direct contractual agreements with vendors.

Communications between library staff and faculty involve numerous links, both formal and informal. A common faculty-initiated communication is a request that the library purchase a specific title; a typical library-initiated communication is a request for advice concerning the value of a contemplated acquisition.

Item Selection

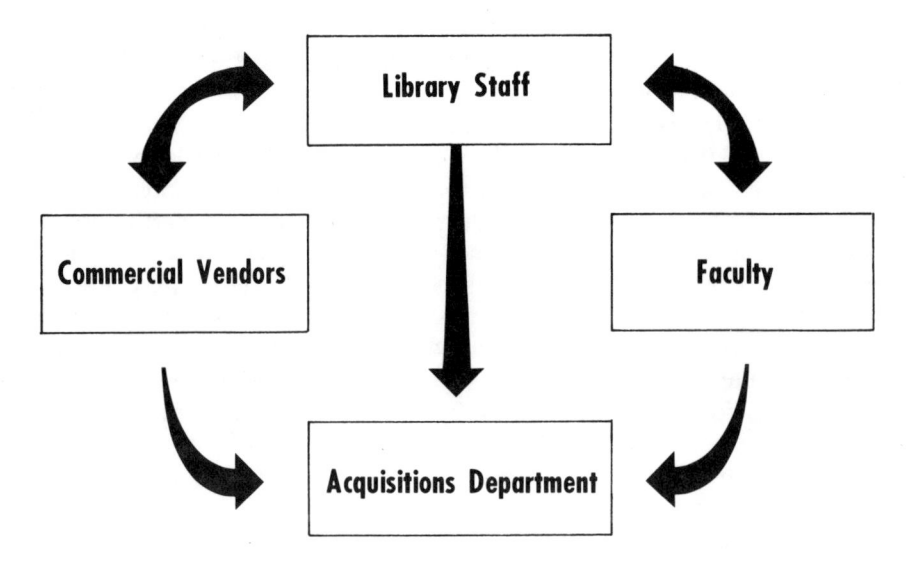

Figure 5-1. Item-Selection Communication Patterns

Among library staff any one or combination of the following may participate in item selection: the library director, the collection-development officer, bibliographers, branch librarians, or reference and other special-collection librarians. Some libraries are now involving staff members in item selection who traditionally have not been active in collection development. For example, members of the cataloging department in two of the institutions studied recently have been assigned selection responsibilities. As the demand for original cataloging decreases with the expansion of shared cataloging systems, more members of cataloging departments may be assigned other duties, on either a part-time or a full-time basis, and item selection is an appropriate assignment.

Faculty play both formal and informal roles in collection development. Those involved formally are designated by their colleagues as faculty-library "liaisons." They work in this capacity either independently or with other colleagues in a faculty-library committee. Typically, department chairpersons are responsible for selecting both library liaisons and committee members. Another common pattern is election to this status by the department faculty. Faculty playing formal roles in collection development are junior members, senior faculty no longer involved in research, or faculty bibliophiles, that is, individuals who have a personal interest in books and collection development.

Not all departments in institutions which use faculty-library liaisons actually fill the position; furthermore, in those which do, liaisons cannot always be relied on to develop collections in support of the interests of all their departmental colleagues. Many tend to select titles in areas of their own interest and expertise.

Faculty informally involved in collection development are persons who submit unsolicited title requests or who are approached by library staff members or faculty-library liaisons for advice concerning a potential acquisition of particular interest to them. Faculty informally participating seldom submit more than a few requests a year, and these are titles in support of their own research and instructional interests. The proportion of faculty informally participating in item selection varies considerably across institutions. In some institutions faculty involvement in item selection is an honored tradition. New faculty quickly become socialized to participate. In other institutions, item selection always has been primarily the responsibility of the library, and few faculty participate.

Faculty involvement varies considerably not only across institutions but also across departments within an institution. Again, tradition and personal interest play a role in shaping the behavior of a department. If a library committee has become an institution in a department, other faculty may let the committee handle all aspects of collection development. On the other hand, if a single person has taken charge of collection development for many years, his or her influence on faculty involvement may persist long after that faculty member retires or leaves.

Gaps may result in those areas of the collections in which the primary responsibility for collection development is with faculty. As has been suggested earlier, the level of faculty participation in item selection varies considerably across faculty, and many faculty limit their item-selection activities to titles consistent with their own interests. Thus, in fields of no current interest to faculty or of current interest to faculty who have little involvement in item selection, collection development may not keep pace with new material which becomes available.

There are different contractual arrangements between libraries and commercial vendors, including standing orders, blanket orders, and approval plans. Standing orders are given to specific publishing houses, most commonly university presses and research institutes. These are continuing orders with the publisher to send one or more copies of every item published.

Blanket orders are contractual agreements between libraries and jobbers, such as Baker and Taylor or Blackwell North American. In blanket orders the library agrees to accept copies of all new titles issued by specified presses, with the exception of those in a few subject areas. Blanket orders may be given to foreign book dealers, such as Harrasowitz in Germany or the Rosenbergs in London.

The approval plan is a contractual agreement with a jobber to send copies of all materials published in specifically defined areas. Presses may or may not be stipulated. The library reviews materials sent and, if inappropriate, returns them to the jobber. To be sure, librarians tend to use the terms *blanket order* and *approval plan* interchangeably and thereby cause confusion.[1]

Libraries usually count on vendors to build the areas of the collection which they are awarded. If it is noticed that an order submitted by a fund administrator should have been supplied by a vendor, the vendor usually will be informed of the oversight. Or if it is noticed that a title seems out of the scope of a blanket order, the item is returned to the jobber. But many libraries neither systematically assess how well vendors cover the areas they are assigned nor question the procedures vendors employ to select titles.

Faculty and librarians dealing with the manifold aspects of item selection rely on many tools for identifying items. Faculty, for the most part, are alerted to titles through citations and reviews encountered in their professional reading, as well as publishers' announcements received through the mail or carried in scholarly journals. Librarians rely on a number of review periodicals for domestic imprints. These include *American Libraries, Library Journal*, and *Publishers Weekly*. The periodical *Choice* offers an additional service. Its reviews are available on 3-by-5 cards which can be sorted and circulated to librarians and faculty. Reviews in all these periodicals tend to be rather brief, and many involved in selection feel that they are too superficial. Nevertheless, these tools are widely used in colleges and universities.

Library of Congress proof slips of forthcoming catalog cards are also used extensively as item-selection tools by librarians. Proof slips are especially useful in identifying new items produced by small or foreign publishing houses. National bibliographies, yet another tool used by librarians, are issued regularly to cite new publications within specified geographical areas. These tend to be comprehensive listings. Many librarians consider *Publishers Weekly* a national bibliography for new domestic issues. Many other materials are employed by librarians, including announcements from publishers, advertisements in scholarly journals, comprehensive bibliographies within specified substantive areas, bibliographies in published articles, and the accessions lists of other academic and research libraries.

Item-Selection Procedures in Seven Academic Libraries

For each of the seven institutions studied, we summarize the selection procedures employed. The summaries identify the principal decisionmakers, assess their relative contributions to item selection, outline each institution's fund structure for acquisitions, and list major tools relied on by the several selection groups.

Earlham College

Item selection at Earlham is accomplished almost entirely by librarians and faculty. Standing orders are maintained with only a few publishers (for example, The Brookings Institution), and these are within carefully defined subject areas. For the most part, vendors are relied on only for their service as distributors, with Earlham faculty and librarians selecting the titles which vendors then supply.

At the beginning of the fiscal year, the librarian divides the budget provided by the college for acquisitions into two parts—one to support continuing subscriptions, the other for the purchase of books and new subscriptions. In 1977-1978, this division was approximately 50 percent for each part. Funds for the purchase of books and new subscriptions are then further allocated to departments, nondepartmental curriculum areas, reference, and general collection development.

Many of the academic program areas designate faculty as liaisons to the library. These persons assume major roles in item selection for their areas. Titles desired by other faculty are typically filtered through liaisons. Some liaisons review requests by colleagues in order to cancel those they consider inappropriate; others monitor requests merely to update encumbrances against their allocations. Once a month the library circulates to liaisons those *Choice* cards consistent with their areas of responsibility. Liaisons may reroute cards to other faculty, but often rerouting is limited to those cards reviewing titles in areas of their colleagues' specific interests.

At Earlham, librarians are responsible for reference and general collection development. They also select titles in support of those academic program areas in which faculty do not actively participate in item selection. Selection in support of these programs involves nearly all the professional staff, with the division of labor being based on academic background and interest. In some areas librarian activity may amount to regularly supplementing the *Choice* card orders returned by liaisons. In others, librarians have assumed the role of faculty representative, receiving directly all *Choice* cards appropriate to the area.

The library director plays a pivotal role in the development of the humanities and social-science collections, supplementing the selections of almost all faculty liaisons and assuming the primary selection role for general collection development as well as several specific academic program areas. Few materials in the social sciences and humanities are ordered without at least a review by the librarian. For books this review is, with few exceptions, a formality. But the librarian exercises considerable influence when new periodical subscriptions are considered. Collection development in the sciences is handled in the same way by the science librarian.

In 1977-1978 about $23,500 was budgeted to the various departments and curriculum areas. Using *Choice* card distribution lists, we estimated that nearly $17,500 was budgeted to areas in which faculty liaisons were designated, and about $6,000 was budgeted to areas in which librarians were the major selectors. Because librarians actively select in support of almost all academic programs and faculty supplement selection in areas in which librarians are the principal selectors, these figures do not completely describe the relative contributions of each group to the building of the collections in support of specific substantive areas. But they do reflect the significant role played by both groups in influencing collection development in support of these areas.

In addition to the college allocation for acquisitions, which in 1977-1978 was nearly $68,000, the Earlham library has access to endowment, grant, gift, and other special funds, most of which have restrictions placed on their use. In 1977-1978, special funds amounted to approximately $40,000, or about 36 percent of the nearly $110,000 spent on acquisitions. Major portions of the special monies came from gifts, totaling about $11,000, and the Earlham School of Religion. The latter fund was nearly $14,000. The disposition of special funds is, for the most part, administered by librarians.

Choice is the major tool used by both faculty and librarians at Earlham to facilitate their selection activities. Both regularly read professional journals, and publishers' announcements also facilitate faculty selection activity, but to a lesser extent. Librarians supplement their review of *Choice* with the review of *Publishers Weekly, Library Journal, The New York Times Book Review, The Chronicle of Higher Education, Science*, and *Human Nature.*

Stockton State College

In contrast with Earlham, collection development which supports specific academic programs at Stockton is accomplished almost entirely by faculty. Librarian activity in collection development is restricted, for the most part, to reference and general collection development. Students at Stockton are encouraged to initiate book requests. Indeed, Stockton is the only library in this book which maintains a separate student book fund. Only monies for book and media purchases are directly allocated to faculty funds. Subscriptions desired by faculty are submitted to the library director, who must approve all new serial commitments. The costs of continuing and new subscriptions are borne by a separate periodicals fund, which in 1977-1978 was budgeted $100,000.

In the 1977-1978 budget, a total of $171,000 was allocated for book purchases. Funds for book orders in support of academic programs accounted for 73 percent of this budget; funds for reference and general collection development accounted for 21 percent of the budget; and the remaining 6 percent was placed in the student book fund.

Book monies allocated for the support of academic programs are distributed among five funds, corresponding to the five divisions of the college. The four major divisions—arts and humanities, natural sciences and mathematics, professional studies, and social and behavioral sciences—are budgeted equivalent amounts. The general studies division is assigned about one-third of the amount given a major division. A faculty member from each division is chosen annually by divisionwide election to serve as the division's library liaison. A library liaison is responsible for administering divisional funds and directing book orders from colleagues to the library's acquisitions staff. Formally, the role of liaisons in selecting titles is no different from that of their colleagues, but in practice liaisons usually contribute the bulk of faculty selections.

The manner in which division funds are distributed among departments within the division is left to the discretion of each division. Some divisions have chosen to apply formulas, distributing money equitably across faculty or departments. Others employ no schemes for reallocation, either because of the interdisciplinary approach of their faculty or because division underspending is common. In the latter case, no reallocation is necessary since money is always available and no request is ever denied.

Also varying across divisions is the level of faculty activity, but in general only a minority of faculty regularly submit orders. Data on faculty involvement at Stockton are difficult to gather, for most requests are forwarded by the division liaisons with no indication of the origin. In one division, it was estimated that 25 percent of the faculty initiate no orders whatsoever. Although the rest occasionally submit orders, only about 5 percent of the division's faculty regularly contribute.

The underlying collection policy of the Stockton library is to acquire titles needed to support current coursework. Reliance on faculty reflects the judgment of the library administration that faculty are in the best position to choose titles supporting their instruction. But the library is also aware of the gaps which result from faculty inactivity and the imbalances which are created by a few unusually energetic item selectors. A new position of collection-development librarian has been established. This individual is the library's primary liaison with faculty concerning collection development.

The collection-development librarian identifies areas of the collection which are weak relative to Stockton's academic program, as well as areas in which resources have been overcommitted. Detection of collection inadequacies is aided by data from Stockton's automated circulation system, which provides a number of indicators of collection use. Faculty still play the major role in item selection, but the collection-development librarian coordinates their activities, keeps them abreast of problems in the collection, and collaborates with them in correcting problems.

The librarians in public services are those primarily responsible for reference and general collection development. Faculty are not solicited for reference or general collection recommendations. Faculty do submit unsolicited suggestions for the general collection, but seldom suggest titles for the reference collections. Public-service librarians are also primarily responsible for spending left-over divisional funds. In 1977-1978, these totaled about $15,000. Unused funds are spent according to the general priorities of the library staff, but these are not necessarily the priorities of the division from whom the allocations were assumed.

Stockton is the only library in our sample to have within its acquisitions-fund structure separate monies for audiovisual materials. This reflects the institution's deeper commitment to nonbook formats. Each of the four major divisions is allocated separate funds for media purchases. The general studies division has no fund for nonbook materials. The library's media-services department is also budgeted monies for acquisitions. In 1977-1978, a total of $23,000 was allocated for media: each division received $4,000, and the media-services department received $7,000. The director of media services administers the department's fund and makes all decisions concerning its expenditure.

The library does circulate to faculty liaisons the latest issue of *Choice*. It also encourages faculty to come to the library to review other tools. But in general, faculty selection is directed by their professional reading and unsolicited publishers' advertisements. Librarians at Stockton rely primarily on standard library tools, for example, *Choice, Library Journal, Publishers Weekly, Books in Print*, and subject bibliographies.

Brown University

At Brown, faculty and reference librarians are those primarily involved in collection development. The reference librarians are responsible for developing both the reference and the general collections. In addition, they share with faculty the responsibility for collection development in support of specific academic programs.

Commercial vendors are involved in selecting or facilitating the selection of some titles for the Brown collection, accounting for about 5 percent of the expenditures on materials in 1977-1978. The plans include a blanket order with Yankee Book Peddler for publications from some twenty university presses; a blanket order with the Rosenbergs for European books and serials in art; an approval plan with Harrasowitz for titles in German language and literature, religion, and mathematics; and an approval plan with Blackwell North American for U.S. and British history books and titles published by university presses not included in the Yankee contract.

The university allocation for book and serial acquisitions is distributed among some fifty funds, about thirty-five of which are earmarked for the purchase of materials in direct support of academic departments and curriculum areas. Remaining funds support continuing subscriptions, library departments, and vendor contracts. The 1977-1978 proposed allocation was about $630,000, of which 24 percent was budgeted to the thirty-five academic programs. About 60 percent of the $630,000 was allocated to the fund for continuing subscriptions. All serials received by the library for more than three years are supported by this fund; academic program funds acquire new subscriptions and support the first three years of their receipt.

In addition to the university allocation, the Brown library has access to numerous other funds, which in 1977-1978 accounted for nearly $200,000 of library acquisitions, or about 25 percent of the library's total expenditure on acquisitions. University support for medical-program acquisitions is budgeted independently of its support for other library acquisitions, and it is considered part of these special funds. Also included among special funds are endowments, one-time gifts to the library, and those portions of research grants earmarked for library acquisitions. As was mentioned in chapter 3, endowments account for almost all the acquisitions of the John Hay Library and the Pembroke Library. Endowments also contribute significantly to academic program purchases, with more than half the departments holding endowments expressly for library acquisitions. In 1977-1978, endowment funds held by departments purchased nearly $18,000 worth of materials.

Both public-service librarians and faculty purchase titles with academic program funds. Indeed, collection development in support of specific programs is based on a partnership between the library and faculty. In this partnership, the library depends heavily on faculty for substantive expertise since few reference librarians have graduate training in areas of their collection activities. Some of the more experienced reference librarians have accumulated much substantive knowledge in their fields of specialization, and consequently they tend to do more item selection. Each of the nine reference librarians is designated collection-development responsibility for several academic programs; departments designate faculty as library liaisons. Both reference librarians and liaisons participate in selection for departments, with the degree of their coordination varying considerably across the partnerships. In 1975, faculty were canvassed to assess their attitudes concerning collection-development procedures. Only four departments desired, and subsequently received, more autonomy in building collections to support their instruction and research; the rest wished to continue the partnership approach.

Item Selection

Reference librarians administer all academic program funds. Faculty requests are filtered through the appropriate fund administrator. As a rule, reference librarians review faculty requests only to monitor expenditures and update their order files; on expensive items they may confer with faculty prior to routing the request to acquisitions.

All fields assigned to a reference librarian fall into one of the following classifications: biological sciences, humanities, physical sciences, or social sciences. For example, one librarian administers funds for economics, education, political science, sociology, and urban studies. Another monitors biology, botany, and psychology. Librarians are assigned areas consistent with their prior training and interests. Since reference librarians have other responsibilities, they are not full-time selectors. Indeed, only about one-third of their time is devoted to collection development. Furthermore, what time they do devote is distributed among a number of subjects. The library is aware of these limitations in its support of collection development, but fiscal constraints preclude devoting more resources to this effort.

The faculty members who serve as library liaisons tend to be the reference librarians' sole contact with other faculty since requests that originate from other faculty are generally funneled through the liaisons. The item-selection roles assumed by liaisons vary. Some are active selectors; others do no more than consult with librarians when advice on a purchase is requested. Some attempt to select titles in support of all areas of department interest; others tend to select only to support their own research and instructional activities.

Well over 50 percent of the titles purchased with academic program funds are the result of reference-librarian selections. The level of faculty-initiated selection varies from department to department, but generally faculty in the humanities are the most active and in the social sciences the least. Although librarians submit the majority of requests, many of their decisions are informed by advice they solicit from faculty. Indeed, some librarians regularly send packets of information about new titles to department representatives, requesting that the titles be ranked according to the importance of their acquisition. This system was particularly common within the sciences.

Generally, in areas in which faculty have shown interest in collection development, reference librarian-liaison communication occurs more regularly. Also, communication regularly occurs in areas in which the assigned reference librarian feels additional substantive expertise is needed. As mentioned in the previous paragraph, some librarians send to liaisons book information in the form of reviews, book lists from journals, and publishers' announcements. But the library maintains no program for distribution of selection aids to all faculty liaisons. Almost all reference librarians monitor *Choice, Library Journal, Publisher's Trade List Annual,*

Publishers Weekly, and *Weekly Record* to facilitate their selections. In addition, each reviews a number of other sources, including scholarly journals directly relevant to their subjects of assigned responsibility.

The Pennsylvania State University

The Pennsylvania State University budget for library acquisitions comprises two basic components: an allocation for University Park libraries and an allocation for the libraries of the commonwealth campuses. The associate dean is responsible for the division of the acquisitions budget into these components and the further assignment of University Park monies to some seventy funds. These allocations are subsequently reviewed and approved by the dean. The coordinator of the commonwealth campus libraries is responsible for allocating campus funds. Although the coordinator sets the level of funding for each campus, she or he takes no part in reallocations at the campus level. Campus-level reallocations are the responsibility of the campuses' librarians. In 1977-1978, the Penn State budget for materials acquisitions was about $1.6 million, with University Park being assigned 77 percent of the monies and the campus libraries assigned 23 percent.

The seventy funds of the University Park libraries fall into three categories: continuing serials commitments; specific academic programs, library departments, or branches; and approval and blanket-order plans. In 1977-1978, the nearly $1.2 million budgeted for acquisitions was distributed among these categories as follows: 61, 26, and 13 percent, respectively.

The blanket-order and approval contracts held by Penn State include both domestic and foreign vendors, with $100,000 being budgeted to domestic and $51,700 to foreign plans in 1977-1978. The major domestic contract is an approval plan with Baker and Taylor for all the publications of specified publishers, except for titles in predesignated areas of minimal interest to Penn State. Well over half the money allocated to foreign vendors is for blanket orders with vendors in Britain, Germany, and the Low Countries.

Item selections for academic programs, library departments, and branches are made by both faculty and librarians. In 1977-1978, 27 percent of the $310,000 allocated to these funds was placed in academic program accounts, 41 percent in Pattee department accounts, and 32 percent in branch-library accounts. Each of these nearly fifty-five funds is assigned to a fund administrator, either a faculty member or a librarian. In most cases the fund administrators are the principal item selectors for materials purchased with their funds. In a few instances, they work with faculty committees. But in all cases, fund administrators must approve the order of titles acquired with the monies in their accounts. Hence, fund administrators and commer-

Item Selection

cial vendors with blanket-order or approval contracts are the groups making most of the selection decisions at Penn State.

Although the monies allocated to their funds can be used only to purchase monographs, fund administrators are responsible for both book and serials acquisitions. In an effort to control serial growth at Penn State, the library does not allocate monies to fund administrators for the purchase of new serials. New serials titles may be acquired only if current serials of equivalent dollar value are canceled. Hence, when fund administrators initiate or approve an order for a new serial, they must also indicate serial titles presently being charged to their areas of responsibility that can be canceled for the required monetary credits.

The academic program funds are associated with curricular areas served by Pattee's general collections in the humanities and social sciences. Faculty administer funds in the program areas in which they have expressed an interest. At Penn State, most faculty administrators are volunteers. They are usually either senior professors who have assumed the responsibility for years or junior faculty members who may be both interested in collection development and motivated to demonstrate a service attitude for their more senior colleagues. Pattee librarians are fund administrators for academic areas in which faculty traditionally have exhibited little interest. Librarians designated as administrators of these monies may come from any department of the library, and typically have been chosen on the basis of their interests and academic backgrounds. Of the twenty-six academic program funds existing in 1978, faculty administered twenty-one.

Branch librarians are fund administrators for ten of the twelve branch-library funds; faculty administer the other two. Pattee librarians administer all Pattee department funds. These include funds for reference, undergraduate materials, special collections, and library services. Also included in this group are funds for Hispanic and Slavic studies, which together were budgeted $20,000 in 1977-1978. Collection development for these programs is the responsibility of two persons designated as bibliographers.

The bibliographers and the collection-development coordinator are the only persons who devote their full attention to University Park's collection development. The bibliographers limit their attention to the area-studies programs they administer. The coordinator's responsibility is broader, defining overall collection goals and objectives. Other fund administrators participate in collection development as only a part-time activity. In many cases, their primary job-related concern has little to do with their collection-development responsibilities.

As observed at other institutions, the level of faculty concern for balance in the orders they submit varies considerably among faculty fund administrators. Furthermore, few faculty are concerned with more than an informal assessment of the strengths and weaknesses of collections. To gain more control over the development of collections for which faculty are primarily responsible, the library is presently designating some staff members as selection liaison librarians. Each liaison is assigned a program area administered by a faculty member; the criterion for assignment is primarily academic background. Liaisons will supplement selections submitted by faculty administrators. They also will be responsible for uncovering and correcting weaknesses in the collections of their concern and for offering consultation to faculty administrators. The pool from which liaison librarians can be chosen includes the entire professional staff. Liaisons will take four hours per week from their normal job responsibilities to assume their collection-development responsibilities.

The library circulates relevant catalogs and publishers' announcements to faculty fund administrators. On request, the library will route other tools such as *Choice* or *Publishers Weekly* to faculty, but few such requests are received. There is a tendency among faculty to ignore the announcements of publishers covered by current vendor arrangements. They assume that these titles will be sent to the library automatically.

The books received on approval or blanket-order plans are put on display in the acquisitions department in Pattee. The entire Penn State community is invited to review these potential acquisitions. In fact, only fund administrators visit the area, and only librarian administrators are regular visitors. Few faculty fund administrators ever review vendor selections, although vendor selections supplement collection development in all academic program areas. It was estimated that about 30 percent of the money spent on vendor plans purchases books in the sciences, 30 percent in the social sciences, and 40 percent in the humanities.

Fund administrators of the commonwealth college libraries are the head librarians of each campus. All item selection is done locally, but all orders are monitored by staff in the acquisitions department at University Park. Using a variety of techniques, most campuses attempt to bring faculty into the collection-development process. Some maintain faculty-library committees which, if not directly involved in selection, at least provide a review and approval mechanism for librarian selections. The collections at the campuses are intended to be "working collections," that is, heavily used materials. The campuses are supposed to rely on the holdings of University Park for titles which would receive minimal use.

The University of North Carolina, Chapel Hill

As mentioned in chapter 3, traditionally faculty have played a dominant role in collection development at UNC Chapel Hill. It is exceptional for any library staff member to take full command of all item-selection decisions for a specific academic program. Of the $1.3 million allocated for materials in 1977-1978, faculty were assigned responsibility for 60 percent, or nearly $775,000; and library staff received 30 percent, or $390,000. The remaining 10 percent was divided between the library administrative board, with 8 percent, and outside vendors, 2 percent.

Monies assigned to faculty are allocated to nearly fifty subject areas, two-thirds of which are housed in the Wilson Library and the remaining one-third in the branches. In 1977-1978, faculty funds buying titles for the Wilson collections received 51 percent of the faculty allocation. The science branches received 34 percent, and the social science and humanities branches received 15 percent.

Each faculty fund is administered by a "book chairperson," a faculty member either elected by colleagues or appointed by the department chairperson. These individuals are given formal authority to spend the money in their funds on books and serials in support of the area they represent. Most book chairpersons diligently exercise their authority, and many regularly consult with library staff members. In a few cases, however, book chairpersons are not very active, and library staff members assume responsibility for the expenditure of these monies. In those branches where faculty have confidence in the librarian's substantive expertise, they tend to relinquish item-selection decisions to the branch head. Otherwise, book chairpersons or a faculty committe maintains the authority to make all final decisions.

As indicated earlier, library staff exercised authority over 30 percent of the 1977-1978 materials allocation. Included under their jurisdiction are funds for the undergraduate library, special collections, bibliographic services, and general services. The last category covers duplicate copies, replacements, completions, and exchanges. The largest allocation under the direction of library staff is for bibliographic services. This library department has a total of six bibliographers, most of whose collection-development responsibilities are defined by geographical and language criteria, that is, Asian, Slavic, Latin American, North American, and Western European. Previously there was one bibliographer for the humanities, but the responsibilities of this position are now shared by two humanities bibliographers, one covering North America and the other covering Western Europe. At the time this study was conducted, the position of Western European bibliographer was vacant. The social-science bibliographer is the only one with a substantively defined area of responsibility. But even the scope of that responsibility is limited geographically, covering primarily social-science materials relevant to North America and secondarily those relevant to the United Kingdom and Western Europe. Almost all bibliographer selections are titles in the humanities and social sciences. However, there is frequent interaction among bibliographers, faculty members, and branch librarians in the sciences. The special skills possessed by bibliographers in obtaining materials from their geographical areas may be called on by any book chairperson or branch head. Several of the bibliographers have staffs to accomplish technical-service functions, such as preorder searches, negotiations with dealers, and cataloging.

The third group involved in item selection at UNC is the library administrative board. Two subcommittees of the board are responsible for decision making on new materials. The first is the research fund committee. Theoretically, expensive research materials relevant to any discipline area may be acquired by monies placed in the research fund. In practice, however, these monies are spent on large sets pertinent to the social sciences and the humanities. The research fund accounted for approximately 4 percent of the acquisitions in 1977-1978. The second committee is the serials committee, which approves all requests for new serials as well as all cancellations. This committee is also responsible for obtaining all general and interdisciplinary serials. This is an active committee which meets monthly, September through April. New serial subscriptions or cancellations are recommended by book chairpersons and library staff. Recommendations for new subscriptions must be justified and approved by three faculty members and the relevant book chairperson. The opinion of most faculty and librarians is that requests for new serials subscriptions are usually approved. The serials committee also accounted for approximately 4 percent of the acquisitions in 1977-1978.

Contracts with vendors are limited at UNC. There are two basic approval plans, one with Blackwell North American for publications of the Oxford and Cambridge university presses and one with the Yankee Book Peddler for university presses in the United States. Both plans are administered and monitored by the library staff. There are two other small approval plans maintained by the English Department.

Both library staff and faculty at North Carolina rely heavily on Library of Congress proof slips as identification aids for new materials. The slips provide a comprehensive double-check against the selections made from other sources, thus minimizing oversights.

As mentioned in chapter 3, the library intends to centralize the processes of selection and acquisition of current monographs. Under the new system, the acquisition of current book publications for Wilson becomes the responsibility of bibliographers in the bibliographic-services department. The academic departments served by Wilson are primarily responsible for retrospective collection development and the selection of highly specialized books. This division of collection-development responsibility also exists among the branches and the departments they serve. The new system of selection responsibility is accompanied by a new system of fund allocation which, in 1978-1979, resulted in transferring some $330,000 from faculty book funds to bibliographer and branch-librarian book funds. Faculty previously controlled over half of the monies allocated for monographs, but under the new system faculty control less than 15 percent of these funds.

University of Wisconsin, Madison

At Wisconsin, bibliographers and branch librarians are the only individuals funded for acquisitions. Of the $747,000 initially budgeted for new monographs in 1977-1978, bibliographers were allotted 50 percent and branches 24 percent. The remaining 26 percent was retained for replacements, reference, reserve materials, and contingencies.

Allocations for new materials can be used only for the purchase of monographs. As at Penn State, Wisconsin has instituted a zero-growth restriction on serials commitments. Branch librarians and bibliographers can purchase new subscriptions only with credits they have accumulated in canceling titles on their active serials lists. In 1977-1978, serials for the general library system cost approximately $900,000. Of this, 61 percent was spent for collections held by the branches and 39 percent for collections housed in Memorial. New-subscription expenditures were split equally between purchases for the branches and purchases for Memorial.

Titles arriving from blanket-order and approval plans accounted for about $80,000, or 10 percent of the money spent on monographs in 1977-1978. Contracts with vendors of these arrangements are negotiated directly by bibliographers and branch librarians, and thus each has limited subject-area or geographical-area coverage. Most of the arrangements presently existing were negotiated by Memorial's bibliographers, and all bibliographer contracts are with foreign concerns. Among the branches, physics maintains several approval plans with both domestic and foreign publishers. Expenditures on blanket orders do not reflect exactly the extent of vendor involvement in collection development. When librarian- or faculty-initiated requests for foreign materials are received by the system's acquisitions department, they are sent to an appropriate vendor holding a blanket-order contract with the library. Hence, expenditures attributed to foreign vendors include supplementary selections by librarians and faculty.

There are no acquisitions funds formally assigned to faculty groups at Wisconsin, but faculty do participate in collection development. This is particularly, although not consistently, true in the development of branch collections. In some branches, faculty are responsible for most of the decisions to acquire titles. In others, the professional-school branches, for example, faculty do no more than submit an occasional request. Typically, where faculty are primarily responsible for selection decisions, branch librarians facilitate the process of collection development by monitoring selection tools and routing materials describing potential acquisitions to faculty members for their review. Since these materials are often the primary tools employed by faculty to select titles, branch librarians who facilitate faculty selection indirectly influence collection development. Only in one branch did the librarian play no role in collection development, neither facilitating faculty selections nor submitting orders on his own.

Faculty participation in the building of collections associated with bibliographers is minimal. Although library liaisons are designated in a number of departments served by branches, there are few liaisons among those departments served by Memorial. What faculty participation does occur is based on informal relationships which have evolved between faculty and bibliographers. For the most part, bibliographers solicit faculty advice only when considering an expensive and narrowly focused research set. Prior to terminating a serial subscription, a bibliographer might contact faculty possibly interested in the title. Faculty contacts with bibliographers seem limited to requests for materials that might require a bibliographer's special skills to acquire. The few requests faculty submit for readily available materials are typically sent directly to the acquisitions department.

Faculty served by branches may be more active in collection development than those served by Memorial because of the physical proximity of the branch collections to the departments they serve. This may result in faculty identifying more strongly with the collections. This feeling of ownership is reinforced in many cases by the origin of branches. Most were originally departmental collections which have only recently become part of the general library system. Finally, there is a perception within the academic community that bibliographers and the heads of the professional-school libraries need to depend less on faculty for subject expertise. Bibliographers and professional-school branch heads frequently have advanced subject training in their fields; and often they are given faculty appointments, an indication of their more collegial position with the faculty.

Bibliographers are primarily responsible for the development of Memorial's reference and special collections. Although the Memorial reference collection has a separate allocation for materials, most of its allotment is spent by bibliographers. The reference staff supplements bibliographer activity; they regularly monitor reference selection tools that may also be covered by bibliographers. Titles purchased for Wisconsin's rare-book room are also the result of bibliographer selections, with the history-of-science bibliographer contributing most. The rare-book collection is not funded separately; selections are purchased with bibliographer funds.

Library of Congress (LC) proof slips are used almost universally as selection tools among bibliographers and branch librarians. In fact, slips appropriate to branch collections are regularly routed from Memorial to the branches. The *Weekly Record* is another tool regularly monitored by a

Item Selection

number of bibliographers and branch librarians. Other commonly used tools include publishers' announcements, new book lists regularly appearing in journals, and book reviews in scholarly publications. National bibliographies are used extensively by the area bibliographers.

University of California, Los Angeles

At UCLA, money available for acquisitions is distributed among about ninety funds. Seventeen of these funds are used to purchase materials for the branch libraries. In 1977-1978, these seventeen funds were allocated 52 percent of the nearly $2.1 million the university initially provided for acquisitions, with the biomedical library receiving about one-quarter of the branch monies. All but a few of the remaining funds are earmarked for the purchase of materials for the university research library (URL). In 1977-1978, money allocated to URL funds amounted to about 34 percent of the total budget. Those few funds not directly associated with branches or URL are held for discretionary spending and general services.

Library staff in the branches are those authorized to spend branch-library monies. Usually that authority is vested in only the branch head. Those authorized to spend money in funds associated with URL include bibliographers, librarians in URL departments, and faculty. Of the initial acquisitions budget of $2.1 million, about $149,000, or 7 percent, was directly assigned to bibliographers; $56,000, or 3 percent, to URL department librarians; and $50,000, or 2 percent, to faculty. In addition to the URL funds directly assigned to these groups, an allocation is made to a fund for the purchase of current books. Monies from this fund acquire any current imprint purchased for the URL, with the exception of current imprints costing more than $65. In 1977-1978, the current book allocation amounted to $271,000, or 13 percent of the total acquisitions budget. Because of the availability of a current-book fund, bibliographers, URL department librarians, and faculty can retain resources directly assigned to them for the purchase of older titles or current expensive imprints.

Sources external to the library further supplement the monies available to URL bibliographers. These include gifts from institutions and individuals or groups as well as portions of grants received by campus research centers and institutes. For example, the Near East bibliographer and the Jewish Studies bibliographer annually receive allocations from UCLA's Near East Study Center. In 1977-1978, money coming from the center was just about twice that available to these bibliographers from their library allocations. Thus, for some bibliographers money from external sources significantly bolsters the resources made available to them by the library.

Faculty authorized to spend URL funds represent departments served by URL. About twenty-five departments designate liaisons to fill this role, with some of the liaisons sharing their authority to spend department allocations with URL bibliographers. Typically, a faculty member serving as liaison has been assigned this responsibility by the department chairperson. Department allocations varied considerably in size in 1977-1978, with the speech department receiving the smallest allocation, $50, and history of science receiving the largest, $8,210.

Monies assigned to bibliographers, faculty liaisons, and librarians in URL departments are used for the purchase of both books and serials. Each fund they administer bears the future cost of commitments initiated with the fund; that is, there is no general fund which will assume the cost of continuing subscriptions. There is a substantial allocation maintaining URL subscriptions initiated prior to 1962. In 1977-1978, it was $185,000, or about 9 percent of the initial acquisitions budget. This fund is controlled by the assistant university librarian for collection development. In addition to maintaining serials, the fund also provides limited resources for ordering general serials titles for which no bibliographer wishes to assume financial responsibility.

The URL current-book fund supports a number of domestic and foreign blanket orders. At UCLA, a blanket order is an allocation to a vendor which is employed for the payment of titles the vendor selects and sends to the library and of titles selected by UCLA and supplied by the vendor. Thus a blanket order is both a means of paying for current imprints selected by bibliographers, faculty book chairpersons, and library staff in URL departments, as well as automatically receiving vendor-selected titles.

A great deal of the selection activity of bibliographers centers on the blanket-order arrangements. Blanket orders cover approximately sixty countries and in 1977-1978 were allocated $175,000, or 65 percent of the fund for current books. Bibliographers are responsible for reviewing vendor selections, returning inappropriate materials, and refining the profiles used by the vendors in their selection decisions. Bibliographers are also responsible for systematically supplementing vendor selections. In many cases, their supplementing is facilitated by the use of national bibliographies. If a vendor works in a country with a national bibliography, UCLA requests that the vendor send the bibliography with each book shipment, noting within the bibliography those titles included in the shipment. Bibliographies are routed to those selectors interested in the scope of a vendor's activities. Bibliographers then mark in these documents those titles the vendor should send in addition to those he has already selected. National bibliographies are available in about two-thirds of the countries in which UCLA maintains blanket orders.

Perhaps because of the presence of twelve bibliographers and blanket-order arrangements which ensure that UCLA automatically receives almost

Item Selection

all essential titles, faculty play only a small part in the building of the URL collection. With the exception of a small number of faculty intensely interested in collection development, faculty served by the URL contribute few book orders. Those faculty designated as library liaisons submit book orders, but their colleagues, in general, rely on them to spend departmental allocations. Indeed, for faculty who are aware of both the availability of their departmental allocation and the URL bibliographer funds, the likelihood of their approaching an appropriate bibliographer to purchase a title they desire is about the same as the likelihood of their approaching the department's book chairperson. Among the branch libraries, faculty involvement can also be described as minimal with a few exceptions. The major exception is a science branch in which faculty are intimately involved in both library policy and collection development.

Among bibliographers, national bibliographies are the most commonly used tools to facilitate selection activities. In addition, bibliographers monitor scholarly journals and specific subject bibliographies. The science-branch librarians rely extensively on LC proof slips and publishers' announcements for their selection decisions. Among item selectors in the nonscience branches, some follow the pattern of bibliographers and others follow the pattern of science branch libraries.

Summary: The Distribution of Authority

To summarize the discussion of item-selection procedures, we return to the theme of distribution of authority. Three groups can be identified as the principal actors in item selection: library staff, faculty members, and commercial vendors. The proportion of the materials budget each is allocated provides a sense of the relative influence of these groups on collection development.

Library staff almost invariably control funds for services—replacements and reserves. They also administer library department funds—reference, exchange, government documents, maps, rare books, and so forth. In our seven institutions, services and library departments accounted for an average of 10 percent of what the libraries got from their parent institutions for acquisitions. Who is allocated the remaining 90 percent of the institutional budget for materials?

For the most part, the remaining funds are those which directly support the research and instructional programs of specific departments and curriculum areas, including the branch-library funds, the geographical-area funds, the department and curriculum funds, and the funds for current-book approval and standing-order plans. Who is authorized to spend these monies?

For each library, we calculated the distribution of these monies among the various item-selection groups. The results are summarized in figure 5-2. In our calculations, we did not include endowments, grants, and other special funds; only money received from the parent institution was considered. Special funds are typically assigned to selectors by virtue of their substantive focus and are not subjected to the resource-allocation process.

The reader may note what appears to be inconsistencies between percentages appearing in the institutional discussions above and those appearing in figure 5-2. These apparent inconsistencies are explained by the exclusion of allocations to library departments (for example, reference) and services (for example, reserves). The reader should also keep in mind that figure 5-2 summarizes beginning-of-the-year allocations as opposed to actual expenditures.

The labels in the first column of figure 5-2 denote categories of funds. In order to simplify the scheme somewhat, both the small student fund maintained by Stockton and the library administrative board fund maintained by North Carolina have been merged with "librarian funds." The "general subscription fund" refers to monies allocated for the automatic support of continuing subscriptions.

One reads the figure as follows: At Earlham College, of the total funds assigned to support academic programs, 52 percent pays for subscription renewals; no money is allocated to standing-order or approval plans; 18 per-

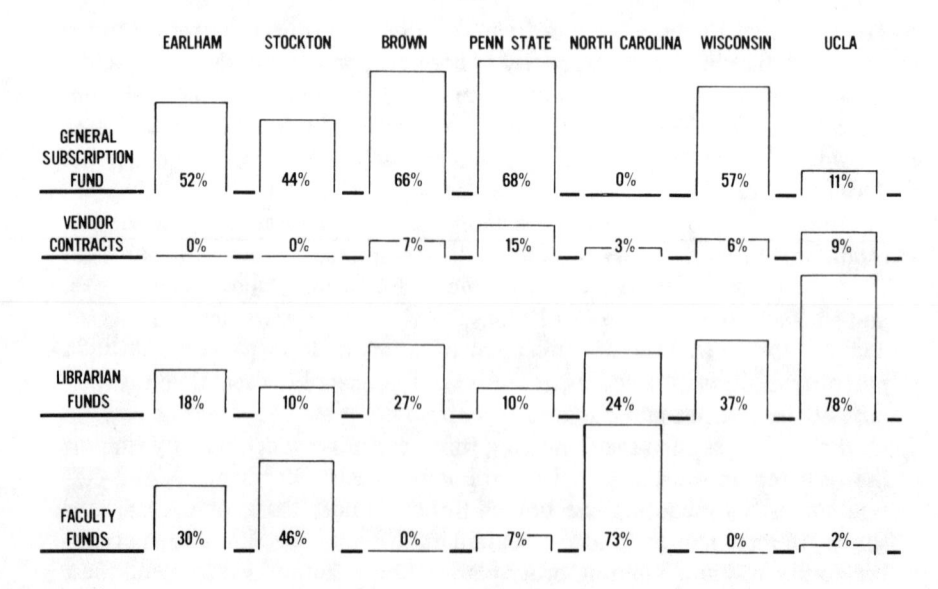

	EARLHAM	STOCKTON	BROWN	PENN STATE	NORTH CAROLINA	WISCONSIN	UCLA
GENERAL SUBSCRIPTION FUND	52%	44%	66%	68%	0%	57%	11%
VENDOR CONTRACTS	0%	0%	7%	15%	3%	6%	9%
LIBRARIAN FUNDS	18%	10%	27%	10%	24%	37%	78%
FACULTY FUNDS	30%	46%	0%	7%	73%	0%	2%

Figure 5-2. Fund Allocation

Item Selection

cent is placed in funds controlled by librarians; and 30 percent is placed in funds controlled by faculty.

From figure 5-2 it can be seen that North Carolina makes no allocation to a general subscription fund, and the UCLA allocation is relatively small, 11 percent. It is not the case that these institutions have minor commitments to continuing subscriptions. In fact, the expenditure data in chapter 4 revealed that both institutions spend approximately 40 percent of their institutional allocation for serials. These institutions do have substantial continuing commitments, but fund administrators are allocated money for serials. Each fund administrator must decide what proportion of his or her serials allocation should be retained for continuing subscriptions and what proportion should be employed for new subscriptions. The UCLA general subscription fund is used to maintain subscriptions started before 1962 and still maintained by the central research library.

Several of the libraries which maintain substantial general subscription funds are phasing them out. Indeed, librarians reported that general subscription funds which automatically support continuing subscriptions are being dismantled by many academic libraries. Apparently, there is a territorial war being waged both outside and inside the library. Humanities and social-science faculty are becoming aware of the fact that serials expenditures in support of the sciences are consuming increasing proportions of available funds; some are pressuring the library to allocate all funds, including those for renewals, by discipline. Bibliographers who note that greater shares of the materials budget drift out each year to the science branches are demanding more stringent control over serials growth. Placing fund administrators directly in charge of monies for continuing commitments provides a mechanism for weeding out unnecessary subscriptions.

In the figure, funds allocated for the support of vendor contracts appear below the general subscription funds. This allows the reader to observe more readily how much money is left after allocations are made to renewals and vendors. Dollars held for these two areas are, in fact, monies committed on the first day of the fiscal year. Hence, what remains of the budget after these allocations is a measure of library flexibility in collection development. Both Brown and Penn State have considerable proportions of their institutional allocation tied up in these first two categories: Brown commits 73 percent to renewals and vendors, and Penn State commits 83 percent.

The last two rows of the figure reflect the variety of item-selection procedures observed at the seven institutions. At Brown, North Carolina, and Wisconsin, librarians play a significant role in the control of research and instruction funds; but at UCLA, the librarians dominate, with 78 percent of the allocation. At Stockton and North Carolina, faculty dominate. At Earlham and Penn State, there is more of a mix. But at Penn State, neither faculty nor librarians are assigned as much money as vendors.

These seven institutions reflect a tremendous variation in the distribution of authority to spend funds. Precommitted funds, that is, subscriptions and vendor contracts, vary from 3 percent at North Carolina to 83 percent at Penn State. Librarian-controlled funds vary from 10 percent at Stockton and Penn State to 78 percent at UCLA. Funds controlled by faculty vary from none at Brown and Wisconsin to 73 percent at North Carolina. Given the fact that these organizations share so many common characteristics in terms of goals, structure, and function, it is amazing that patterns of resource allocation reveal such diversity.

Item Selection in Six Disciplines

In this section we examine the roles of faculty, librarians, and vendors in developing collections for six disciplines: biology, chemistry, English, history, psychology, and sociology. Although we collected data in other disciplines as well, at each campus we spoke to both faculty and library staff about the collections in these disciplines. The analysis presented here allows us to look at similarities and differences in item-selection practices across disciplines. In the discussion, we pair the disciplines by sciences, humanities, and social sciences.

By way of introduction, we describe several ways in which library collections are organized. Most often holdings for the humanities and social sciences are centralized in the campus's main library facility. If there is any distribution of the collection among different facilities, most often science holdings are found apart from the central collection. Art, music, the undergraduate collection, and libraries supporting professional schools (for example, business, education, law) are the only nonscience collections commonly found outside the humanities and social-science core. The typical branch unit maintains and develops a collection for one academic department. Usually the branch head is the only professional librarian within the unit, and the library is housed within the building occupied by its primary users.

Among the seven libraries are three patterns of collection. The first describes only Stockton State College, where the entire collection is housed in one facility. The second pattern is found at Earlham College and Brown University. In both institutions the science collections are physically separated from the social-science and humanities collections, but they are not distributed across the campus in a number of branches; rather, they are housed together in one facility. Brown was one of the first universities in the nation to centralize its science collections. Until the late 1930s, Brown supported a number of departmental libraries in both the physical and biological sciences. First, all the physical-science collections were centralized and sub-

Item Selection 119

sequently the biological-science collections. In 1971, these two independent divisional libraries were finally consolidated in a new building.

Representing the third pattern are Penn State, North Carolina, Wisconsin, and UCLA, which have centralized social-science and humanities holdings and numerous branches, ranging in number from seven at Penn State to fourteen at Wisconsin. At each institution, resources allocated to branch units serve primarily the sciences. However, on these campuses, a variety of nonscience fields are also served by branches, including architecture, art, business, education, law, library science, music, psychology, social work, state and local government, and urban planning.

Several phenomena accompany the dispersed branch structures which characterize Penn State, North Carolina, Wisconsin, and UCLA. The first is the difficulty in containing overlap in collection holdings, particularly among the science units. Of course, some overlap in branches is desirable, indeed absolutely necessary, but many librarians feel that it could be more effectively controlled. For example, from one perspective, chemistry is a middle ground between physics and mathematics; but from another perspective, chemistry bridges biochemistry, bacteriology, botany, and biology. If there are branches in any of these fields, independent of a chemistry branch, there will inevitably be collection overlap. To be sure, almost anything that a chemistry library would purchase could be of interest to scholars in one of these other fields. Thus, in a branch structure, duplication of collection is inevitable, as each branch attempts to fill the library needs of its primary users.

Since consolidation might result in more efficient collection development, one may question why branches are not merged. The main reason, of course, is the convenience which the branch library affords its primary user group. Faculty strongly support the placement of library materials close to their offices. In fact, when one considers the faculty pressures to maintain branches, it is surprising how much centralization exists on large university campuses. A critical factor determining the extent of centralization of holdings is the size of the campus. It would be virtually impossible, for example, to locate one facility at the University of Wisconsin which could conveniently serve all faculty in the sciences.

A second phenomenon accompanying dispersed branches is the emergence of gaps in the collections. Because of the constraints on acquisitions budgets, librarians are reluctant to purchase materials peripheral to the interests of their primary user group. Even materials which may be of direct interest are sometimes bypassed if they are perceived by librarians or faculty to be more directly consistent with the collection-development responsibilities of another branch library. Interdisciplinary areas are most susceptible to gaps in library collections. For example, environmental sciences could justifiably be among the collection-development responsibilities of a number of branches, including chemistry, engineering, and biology. At one of the universities studied, there is no critical mass of faculty interest in environmental sciences within any one department. Although there is great interest distributed among many departments, no branch library in the system is comprehensively collecting in support of environmental science. Interdisciplinary programs in new fields are particularly susceptible to this kind of problem.

In university libraries with branches, there is usually little formal coordination among branches to minimize either overlap or the creation of gaps in the collections. Librarians may be informed by the acquisitions department if a title they order has already been acquired by another branch. A librarian's response to this information depends on a number of factors, including the distance of the existing copy from the branch's primary user group, the cost of the item, and the anticipated response of faculty if a copy is not available at a branch. But coordination on more than a title-by-title basis is rare. Little effort has yet been devoted to defining systemwide collection-development goals in such a way that unwanted gaps are avoided and duplication is minimized. Occasionally branches informally designate areas in which collection building will or will not occur, but such arrangements are the result of personal negotiation.

Although there is much variation in the specific collection problems which accompany branch structures, one common problem is the relationship of science-branch collections to the undergraduate library collection. Science branches usually build collections in support of research, and materials supporting instruction are given very low priority. Furthermore, the space in many branches is so limited that it is impossible to allow use by lower-division students and still retain satisfactory library services for faculty and graduate students. Hence, in some branches use of the facility by first- and second-year students is actively discouraged. It is assumed by many branch librarians that the undergraduate library should support the science-material needs of first- and second-year students, but in universities the collection development of science materials in the undergraduate library is minimal. Undergraduate libraries traditionally maintain basic social-science and humanities collections. The undergraduate librarians interviewed were sensitive to the inadequate resources for undergraduates taking science courses, but there was no consensus on remedies. There seemed, however, to be strong agreement among undergraduate library heads and many science branch librarians that the division of responsibilities between branch libraries and the undergraduate library was indeed in need of clarification.

Typically, only the branch head and faculty immediately served by the branch are involved in collection development for that unit. The central collection is typically built by reference librarians, bibliographers, and faculty served by the central collection. In comparison to those designated bibliographers, branch librarians have less academic training consistent with their collection-development responsibilities. Three factors contribute to this. First, within the library profession, academic strength in the social sciences and humanities exceeds strength in the sciences. It is more probable that an individual with the master's degree or Ph.D. in history or English will enter the profession than an individual with a comparable degree in chemistry or physics. Second, branch librarians typically have more contact with their clientele than do those assigned collection-development responsibilities for the central library. Thus they can rely more on interactions with faculty to aid in item selections than can those collecting for the central facility. The relatively less frequent interaction between faculty served by and bibliographers building the central collection is offset by the greater substantive expertise of bibliographers.

Third, new terminology and new fields grow at a faster rate in the sciences than in the humanities and social sciences. Thus it is exceedingly difficult for someone not on the forefront of research to keep pace. Even harder is maintaining the knowledge needed for effective choices in all subfields of a scientific discipline. Hence, it is often assumed that librarians without graduate training in the sciences may be quite as effective in facilitating the selection of materials as are librarians who have had such training.

Although branches tend to be closer to their user groups, faculty involvement in collection development at the branch level varies just as much as faculty involvement with the central collection. There does seem to be a tendency for faculty to relinquish control of collection development when they perceive that expertise exists on the library staff, at either the central facility or the branch. But such competence in the library does not always result in the withdrawal of interested faculty. For example, in one institution a branch head was hired who had considerably more academic expertise than had previously been available. The department served by this unit had a long tradition of faculty involvement in collection development. The importation of expertise did not result in any abdication on the part of the faculty.

Although there is a tendency to rely on expertise when it is available, one cannot expect greater faculty activity simply because expertise is not available. Several factors are at work here: faculty apathy, vendor plans which can compensate for lack of library subject expertise and provide almost all materials requested by faculty, and librarians' acquisition of competence in a field which develops over time, thus permitting rational and effective selection decisions.

It does seem, though, that as a collection's identification with a user group declines, so does the level of faculty involvement in both its development and its use. The largest consolidation of collections is, of course, in the central library. Hence, these collections are most prone to the lowest levels of user identification. Libraries employ a number of mechanisms to reverse this phenomenon. Departmental funds are one such device. These are employed at all libraries included in this book except Wisconsin. The designation of faculty-library liaisons is a second mechanism to connect the user group with library collections. A third device is bibliographer interaction. This mechanism is much less formal than departmental funds and faculty liaisons, and frequently much less successful. As a group, bibliographers vary considerably in their level of communication with faculty. Some bibliographers have part-time teaching appointments and perceive the faculty as their professional peer group. Indeed, they are closer to faculty in academic departments than they are to their library colleagues. Other bibliographers have only a few well-developed contacts among the faculty. These persons spend most of their time within the confines of the library, interacting with other bibliographers, publishers' representatives, and vendors.

Reading rooms, book collections administered independently of a campus library system, often reside within departments in the humanities and social sciences. These small collections knowingly duplicate holdings available in other units on the campus. Reading rooms are pragmatic responses to needs which the library system often cannot readily fulfill:

1. The need for immediate access to frequently used reference materials and journals
2. The need to have a quiet place to study and read, conveniently located near one's office
3. The need for a mechanism which allows reserved materials to be made available quickly to students, with as litle red tape as possible

As library holdings relevant to a faculty group become physically more distant, or as these holdings become more difficult to retrieve because they reside in larger collections, the needs listed above become more acute. The availability of a dedicated branch close to those served by the holdings discourages the evolution of a reading room.

Reading rooms typically develop in an ad hoc manner. Various faculty donate materials to a growing accumulation until some organization of the volumes is necessary to provide convenient access. Departmental funds may be used to obtain clerical help in organizing and maintaining the collecton. Once the collections take on such a "librarylike" demeanor, departments may be tempted to enrich the collections further by allocating funds for major journal subscriptions.

Except for the purchase of often-used reference materials and journals, acquisitions for reading rooms tend to be minimal. The rooms are often maintained by students or part-time help. A reading room may approach the sophistication of a library if grant money is obtained for its support. Such support usually occurs when a faculty member obtains outside funds for research and the budget includes provision for library materials. Frequently faculty decide to divert such grant money to their departmental reading room rather than to the central library, because to do otherwise results in relinquishing control over the items acquired. In one institution a professor had just received a sizable grant which would support the purchase of many titles relevant to an interdisciplinary program. Had these funds been relinquished to the library, because of the interdisciplinary nature of the purchases, the titles would have been dispersed throughout the system rather than gathered in one collection. The professor was considering establishing a reading room in order to ensure that the collection would remain centralized in one facility.

Biology collections in the seven libraries studied are housed in accordance with the patterns summarized at the beginning of this section. Stockton's biology collection is a section of the main library facility. At Earlham and Brown, biology takes up a significant part of the science library collections. Biology holdings at Penn State are within the main library and part of a discrete collection serving agriculture in addition to the biological sciences. At North Carolina, biology is served by independent branches in botany and zoology, but at the University of Wisconsin the botany and zoology collections are housed together in one branch. Finally, at UCLA biology is included in the largest branch in the system, which serves the schools of medicine, dentistry, nursing, and public health; the UCLA hospital and clinics; and the life-sciences division. This branch is also a regional library in the national medical-library network.

The patterns of organization of chemistry collections are similar to those in biology. With the exception of Penn State, chemistry collections in the universities with branch units are dedicated to the support of one department. At Penn State, chemistry is a branch, but the branch is not devoted exclusively to chemistry. It also serves the departments of physics, astronomy, and chemical engineering.

In the chemistry and biology branches, the following mix of faculty-library involvement in collection development was observed. In two of the chemistry libraries, the branch heads were those most responsible for selecting titles. In the other two, faculty dominated in selection decisions. In the biology libraries, the same distribution occurred, but not in the same institutions. Thus, it is not necessarily the case that in a given institution faculty dominance in chemistry implied faculty dominance in biology. For the most part, where faculty were active in collection development, librarians played an active role in facilitating item selection by faculty. There was one exception, a branch in which the librarian took absolutely no part in any collection-development activities. To facilitate faculty selection, librarians route to faculty members titles of potential interest, expecting those titles desired by faculty to be returned with a request for ordering. In some of the branches, the facilitative role was thoroughly institutionalized, with well-established procedures for information dissemination and networks of faculty contacts.

In all cases where a biology or chemistry collection was housed with collections serving other departments or schools, the library took the dominant role in collection development. But it should not be assumed that merely mixing collections results in a lessening of faculty involvement. Indeed, in one branch serving a number of departments in the sciences—not biology or chemistry—the librarian had little involvement in item-selection decisions.

For both biology and chemistry, funds for materials are primarily consumed by serials, and continuing commitments are responsible for most of this consumption. But item-selection activity does not center on serials acquisitions. For both biology and chemistry, the number of new serials titles added during the fiscal year is far below the number of new monographs added. Thus, the number of item-selection activities and decisions involving monographs far exceeds the number involving serials. However, because of the continuing fiscal commitment entailed by a new serial, a subscription decision typically takes more time and involves more individuals than does a decision to purchase a monograph.

In all the institutions studied, the English and history collections are housed in the main library. Item selections for collections in English and history are made with input from three different sources. The first involves faculty. Usually a departmental book chairperson or book committee reviews requests, which may originate from either the faculty or the library staff. The second source is library staff in the main library, typically reference librarians or bibliographers. Bibliographers are rarely assigned specifically to English or history. More often, bibliographers are assigned a geographical area, an historical period, or a discipline cluster, such as the humanities. Therefore, collection responsibilities in both English and history may be divided among several bibliographers. Bibliographers may contact faculty, seeking advice on selection decisions. In most institutions, several faculty members in both English and history are bibliophiles who interact regularly with the bibliographers. The third source of input to item selection is the outside contractors who select materials according to instructions supplied by persons on the library staff—either bibliographers or reference librarians. Faculty may be involved in monitoring or approving the titles supplied by vendors, but this is rare.

Monographs, including retrospective titles, make up the bulk of acquisitions in support of English and history programs. However, retrospective monograph acquisitions are decreasing in academic libraries. In fact, the trend data presented in chapter 4 suggest that the acquisition of all monographic materials, both current and retrospective titles, has been declining in academic libraries.

Turning to the collections supporting psychology and sociology, we note that all such collections are housed in the central facility, with the exception of one branch in the UCLA system which supports both psychology and education. Item selection in psychology and sociology follows the patterns observed for English and history. However, faculty involvement in item selection is typically weaker in both psychology and sociology, and vendor plans tend to be much more prominent.

Collections in the social sciences rely on both journals and monographs. In this regard, psychology and sociology lie somewhere between the sciences and the humanities with respect to their reliance on monographs and serials. With the exception of materials supporting historical studies, materials perceived as useful by social scientists are current materials and are, therefore, more suitable for vendor plans. Furthermore, the social scientists generally tend to use fewer foreign-language materials than scholars in the humanities. However, it should be pointed out that in many subareas of sociology and psychology, scholars use library materials to a far lesser extent than do their colleagues in the sciences and the humanities.

In their research and instructional activities, many social scientists rely heavily on the use of files of numerical data generated through surveys and experiments. Academic libraries are becoming increasingly involved with the collection and maintenance of these files which are frequently in machine-readable form for input to computers. These numerical data files cover a wide range of substantive topics, for example, materials from various government agencies such as the Bureau of the Census and the Social Security Administration, copies of data from nationwide sample surveys, and sets of time-series data of economic indicators. These materials are collected from sources which are new to librarians and require the establishment of a different network of suppliers. Furthermore, the compilation, cleaning, documentation, cataloging, and, most importantly, the analyses of these data sets involve types of activities not yet familiar to most librarians. The collection of computer data files presents a novel challenge, namely the necessity to train librarians in the use of additional skills and knowledge.

The following general remarks pertain to all six disciplines and concern the tools used by both faculty and library staff to facilitate title selection. Reviews of books are printed in professional and scholarly journals long after the titles have been published. Librarians choosing titles in the sciences indicate that they cannot wait for a book to be reviewed in a journal before placing an order. Hence, those making decisions to purchase science titles are often buying on the basis of title alone. Cues which they use include the appropriateness of the title; the reputation of its author, authoring group, editor, or institution of origin; and the reputation of its publisher. In fields outside the sciences, librarians have a more catholic attitude concerning the use of review literature. Those involved in selection in the social sciences and the humanities tend to buy on the basis of title alone only when they feel confident about their competence in the area of selection.

In all disciplines, librarians are alerted to titles mainly through publishers' announcements or lists of "books received," published by scholarly journals or journals within the library profession. Particularly for foreign titles, many national bibliographies are quite comprehensive and hence are relied on extensively.

Faculty rely on few tools to aid in selection other than their own professional reading and publishers' announcements, which bombard them constantly. With one exception, none of the institutions we visited had a system for circulating to faculty on an institutionwide basis information concerning potential acquisitions. Whatever alerting did occur was likely to be the result of a few library staff members interacting with a few interested faculty members.

Conclusion

At the beginning of chapter 4, six questions were raised concerning the planning and implementation of resource allocation in academic libraries. By way of summarizing the last two chapters, we now return to these questions and present responses based on the material discussed thus far. The six questions posed earlier are the following:

1. What planning process is used by an academic library to analyze its environment and resources and subsequently select goals for collection development defined in terms of present and future needs?
2. What is the implementation process by which resources are allocated to achieve these goals?
3. How are the planning and implementation processes related?
4. What procedures are employed to assess the planning and implementation processes?
5. What problems characterize the management of these processes?
6. What improvements can be recommended that may be generalized to other academic libraries?

These questions, adapted from those used by Bower in a study of corporate planning and investments, were a point of origin for our case studies.[2] The questions focus attention on the dual processes of planning and implementation and their interrelationship. With respect to planning activities, in all seven libraries studied there is a common concern for more fully articulated goals for collection development. In most of the institutions, this concern gives rise to the production of written collection-development statements, which are usually prepared in detail for each area of research and instructional activity which the library supports. Usually, collection-development statements specify the level of comprehensiveness to be attained in each area. These may range from a minimal collection designed to support undergraduate instruction to a comprehensive collection designed to support advanced research. For the latter, the library may attempt to acquire a copy of every item available that is relevant to a field.

Collection-development statements vary in degree of specificity, but all statements attempt to delineate the instructional and research needs of the user communities and specify with some degree of rigor the factors to be used in deciding which materials will be added to the library's collection. They may limit collection areas by substantive topic, historical period, geographical area, or language of publication. For example, a policy statement in sociology may specify that comprehensive collections will be maintained in social theory, research methods, social stratification, and medical sociology; that collections appropriate for undergraduate instruction will be maintained in the sociology of religion, social deviance, and political sociology; and that materials will not be collected in the sociology of law, sociology of education, and demography. Such a statement might further indicate which foreign-language publications will be acquired. Collection-development statements usually specify the relative emphasis on current as opposed to retrospective materials. Some collection-development statements are initiated by the library staff and passed on to the faculty for review, revision, and approval. In other instances, they may be prepared with initial input from both the library staff and faculty members.

Collection-development policy statements were certainly the vogue of the late 1970s in academic libraries. Librarians differ in their opinions as to the utility of such statements. Most feel these statements are of minimal value in making specific item-selection decisions. However, all agree that the preparation of such statements is a most informative exercise for both the library staff and the faculty. The specification of current areas of interest among faculty for both research and instructional purposes makes much clearer to all involved what priorities should be maintained in collection development. In addition, many librarians report that such statements can be most useful for defensive purposes if they are challenged by the faculty or other librarians for the inadequacy of their collection-development activities. At present, the planning process for collection development is receiving much systematic attention from most parties involved.

Although it is possible to report considerable productive activity in the area of planning collection development in academic libraries (question 1 above), we did not, in the course of these case studies, encounter a comparable range of activities that would aid specifically in the implementation of the collection-development plans (questions 2 and 3). The activities described in this chapter and chapter 4 comprise the implementation processes, and by now the reader certainly should be convinced of the amazing diversity of implementation practices. However, a great deal of this bustling activity is not yet in accord with collection-development plans.

With respect to the assessment of planning and implementation procedures (question 4), there are several activities to be reported. The first is the attempt on the part of several large university libraries to describe their current collections. With initial leadership from the University of California, Berkeley, a number of academic libraries have now completed a count of their holdings separately for each Library of Congress classification. These libraries are in a position to compare the relative commitments they have made to different subject areas with the collection-development goals stated in their written plans. In addition, these counts provide participating libraries with an opportunity to compare the size of their collections by subject category. However, these shelf-list counts address only the question of relative commitment and overall size. They do not provide information, for example, on the proportion of current versus retrospective or English versus foreign-language materials. Nevertheless, the counts are a first step in the assessment of academic-library collections.

Another important activity is the collection analysis project operating under the direction of the Office of Management Studies (OMS) of the Association of Research Libraries. Through the use of self-study materials and with guidance from the OMS staff, each participating library will review its collection-development policies and practices, with a view toward improving their effectiveness and rationality.

In our opinion, four problems characterize the management of both planning and implementation activities in collection development (question 5). First, the performance of academic libraries in collection development can be assessed along two dimensions: the acquisition of materials to fulfill the needs of present users and of future users. The library can look to faculty and students, the primary user community, for indications of success on the first dimension. But evaluation of performance as it relates to future demand is more problematic. At least for research libraries, this second aspect of performance is more critical than the fulfillment of present needs, since the damage resulting from failure to build for future demand may be irreparable.

The availability of material which supports scholarly endeavors is not indefinite. Indeed, in some countries if material is not immediately acquired shortly after publication, it becomes impossible to acquire through normal marketing channels. The library usually can recover from having missed recently published material in demand by present users. But as time goes on, the likelihood of retrieving publications of the past diminishes, and the expense of retrieval climbs rapidly. The problem of recovering from past mistakes is confounded if entire areas of the literature systematically have been ignored, areas which later become active research interests of the library community.

A second problem characterizing the processes of planning and implementation stems from the observation that collection-development statements are issued with little attention to projected funding levels for materials acquisitions. This may result in expectations on the part of library staff, faculty, and institutional administrators which cannot be met.

A logical next step for academic libraries that have fully articulated collection-development plans and accurate assessments of current holdings would be to make cost projections for different substantive classifications. It is possible to estimate with some accuracy the future costs of serials and monographs required to attain the goals for collection coverage as specified in the collection-development plans. A summary of all these estimates could be used for projecting materials budgets for future years. These projections could be prepared for both subject classification and format of materials. In none of the seven institutions studied has this step been taken. It is certainly our impression that very few, if any, other academic libraries have yet made such detailed projections.

After reviewing several of the collection-development statements completed by the seven institutions, we get the distinct impression that the total funds needed to attain the stipulated collection-development goals would exceed by at least several times any projected materials budgets. Basically, the statements profess a desire to maintain present collection strengths and weaknesses. But the present strengths are primarily the result of collection building which occurred when money for acquisitions was far more plentiful. The 1970s have ushered in a new fiscal environment for libraries. Although academic librarians seem well aware that not all the strengths their collections once harbored can still be maintained, their collection-development statements do not reflect this awareness.

Whether libraries should or should not respond indiscriminately to the demands placed on their resources by faculty and students is a debatable issue. But one can say with certainty that few libraries can respond indiscriminately to all user demands—they just do not have the money to do so. Hence priorities must be established. This brings us to the third management problem—establishing priorities for the resource demands of present users and doing so in the highly political atmosphere of academia.

Faculty, for the most part, anticipate that the library will continue to provide the types of materials and services to which they have become accustomed. On the other hand, the institution's administration expects the library to conduct its activities with diminishing fiscal resources and looks to the faculty for feedback concerning how well the library is doing.

Under these conditions, the librarian is forced to operate in a highly political fashion. Priorities are determined by the "wheels which squeak the loudest." Faculty who are politically active will be more effective in gaining support for their programs, and those who are less effective in lobbying for support or not inclined to participate in such activities will have to contend with the diminishing resources. But political power bases in the academic world frequently shift, and a librarian's allies are unlikely to remain in powerful positions indefinitely. Thus, the political reality of academic life results in not only overall institutional goals becoming secondary to those of politically powerful faculty, but also administrative upheavals if the library has not been exceedingly alert in allocating resources to various factions on campus.

The fourth and final management problem also concerns priority setting, but priority setting relative to future demands. As was suggested earlier, academic libraries, particularly research libraries, are often compelled to collect now for potential future demand. In effect, their collection-development decisions today determine how collections can be used tomorrow.

The actual demand placed on library resources by future users is shaped by decisions made by the academic institution's senior administrative staff and faculty. They make decisions which phase out programs, such as Slavic studies, or establish new programs, such as transportation studies. They make decisions which result in hiring senior faculty who may bring with them areas of research new to the campus.

Because of the need for developing collections for new programs, one would expect senior administrative staff and faculty to be in constant communication with the library concerning various directions the institution is planning to take. But this is not the case. Furthermore, the academic institution is not organized in such a way that librarians can efficiently gather this information on their own. As a result, librarians conduct their collection-development activities for the most part uninformed by the plans or decisions which determine future demands on the collections.

Finally, what improvements can be recommended that may be generalized to other academic libraries (question 6)? Academic librarians need additional support, both from administrators who understand the problems of academic libraries and from faculty members who have sensible and realistic expectations of library performance. More financial support would, of course, alleviate some immediate problems. But administrative support from the institution is needed if libraries are to address the kinds of problems presented here.

Notes

1. Norman Dudley, "The Blanket Order," *Library Trends* 18, no. 3 (January 1970):318-327.

2. Joseph L. Bower, *Managing the Resource Allocation Process: A Study of Corporate Planning and Investment* (Boston: Harvard University, 1970).

6 Organizational Theories and Social Change

The perspective of resource allocation in complex organizations led us at each site to be both restrictive and inclusive. We restricted our attention to those phenomena within the organizational entity known as the central library system and focused our fieldwork on all units within that library system pertinent to collection development. Yet we also included faculty, administrators, and vendors who interact with library staff in collection-development activities. Chapter 3 provided general descriptions of the seven organizations thus identified. Chapters 4 and 5 maintained the organizational viewpoint, although their contents focused on the two processes central to collection development, fund allocation and item selection.

In this chapter we continue our organizational motif, but the discussion is both more general and more synthesized and therefore similar to that of chapter 1. Here we bring together data collected at each site as they relate to five theoretical formulations that occur in the context of all complex organizations: social change, bases of authority, professionalism, organizational boundaries, and conflicting goals. These issues are certainly not the only ones that students of complex organizations have examined, and their importance, as reflected in the quantity of discussion they have provoked among social scientists, varies considerably. We did not begin our fieldwork with these specific issues in mind. Rather, in the course of our work they emerged as fruitful frames for much of the data we were uncovering.

Libraries and the profession they define are making many rapid and fundamental adjustments to new conditions. Although many of the transformations may be judged inevitable, frequently librarians, like many other professionals, resist change. As social scientists, we have an opportunity to provide a different perspective on some of the impediments to timely and effective innovation. In this chapter, therefore, we complement our analyses of theoretical issues with a discussion of the barriers to change and adaptation in academic libraries and their attendant policy implications.

Organizational Theories

Social Change

Change is a fundamental and perennial issue in all social-science disciplines. Theorists—ancient and modern—have considered the causes, processes, and consequences of transformation of social collectivities. Nevertheless, comprehensive and useful theories that adequately explain the phenomenon at either the organizational or the societal level have not emerged yet. Nonetheless, many believe that drastic and continuous alterations in social organization may be the most prominent characteristic of the future.[1]

All organizations change over time. Thus, had we conducted the case studies of these seven academic libraries ten years ago, our report would have been different in many respects, as would a report of 1988 findings. What causes these changes and with what consequences?

During our interviews, we consistently asked senior staff members to describe major changes that academic libraries have experienced during the post-World War II period. Three were repeatedly called to our attention. The first concerns the rate and nature of library acquisitions. Libraries, of course, have had to face head-on the knowledge explosion. Accompanying the explosion has been a concomitant proliferation in both the amount and the types of materials libraries have been called on to collect. The explosion has also encouraged the expansion of services which libraries are called on to provide. In addition to books and periodicals, libraries must now accommodate technical reports, article reprints, newsletters, looseleaf services, government documents, microforms, audiovisual materials, and machine-readable data bases. Also computer-based information retrieval now complements the traditional reference activities of numerous academic libraries.

A second change often noted was in the amount of financial support available to academic libraries. From the 1940s until the late 1960s, there was steady growth in the money available for new materials. But corresponding to the pattern of the U.S. economy generally, the purchasing power for these resources has declined, particularly during the 1970s. Projections generally foresee only stable or declining budgets for academic libraries in the next decade.

The final commonly noted change was the introduction of automated systems to aid in accomplishing several of the principal functions of academic libraries. Computers can now be used to assist in the execution and monitoring of acquisitions, cataloging, circulation, and some reference services. Almost all academic libraries have been affected in some way by automation, and computers will play an increasingly important role in library operations.

While conducting these case studies, we observed three related phenomena: the incremental nature of organizational change, resistance to organizational change, and the discrepancy between potential and actual change. Because of the inherent tendency of organizations to protect themselves in the interest of stability, most social change occurs only incrementally; that is, changes occur gradually and usually have different effects on departments or subunits of the organization. Of course, major changes can and do occur within a very short time. But even in such cases, there is likely to be a period of anticipation of and preparation for change, followed by a period of adjustment.

The application of computer technology to academic libraries illustrates incremental change very well; that is, none of the institutions studied has attempted to automate all functions in the library simultaneously. Although most have plans for attaining an integrated computer system for many functions, each intends to automate serially. Academic libraries could provide automated support for acquisitions, cataloging, circulation, and reference; but they tend to focus their limited resources on one or perhaps two functional areas at any given time.

An aversion to innovation is a universal phenomenon in organizations, and theorists have pointed to both its positive and its negative consequences. A degree of resistance to change is functional for organizations, for it serves as a defense mechanism against the chaos that might accompany change undertaken too rapidly. Nevertheless, resistance must be kept in balance, for an organization that obstructs all change may find itself diverging from its environment. Academic libraries are interesting in their organizational resistance to change, particularly to technological change.

Traditionally, persons who have been attracted to the profession of librarianship have identified with the scholarly activities and tools of the profession. They frequently describe themselves as people who love books and label as "bookmen" those who have a vast knowledge of both the physical properties and the content of books. It is a term conveying strong and positive approbation. To be called a bookman is a mark of honor, and it expresses the traditional essence of the profession. But among those attracted to librarianship, there is a small, but growing, minority who feel comfortable with the knowledge required to understand, design, and operate computer systems. The world of books and the world of computers are perceived as vastly disparate ones. Consequently, many academic librarians resist increasing automation activities.

The third phenomenon we observed concerning change in academic libraries involves the difference between actual and potential social change. Here again, we point primarily to the area of technology. The development of new technological capabilities and their effective operation in organizations always lag. At any given time, the capacity of available technology exceeds current practice. For example, modern large-scale digital computer systems can now accomplish a wide variety of the information acquisition, storage, and retrieval tasks common to academic libraries, but the necessary capital investment for equipment, operating systems, and personnel trained to install and operate these systems is not readily available. Moreover, we noted during our interviews a common resistance even to discussing the implementation of such systems.

As a by-product of computer-aided production systems, many new books and journals are available in both printed and digital formats. To our knowledge, no academic library is yet collecting copies of the magnetic tapes which contain the digital versions of new publications. The equipment for retrieving information from magnetic-tape records of books and journals is not yet adapted to the needs of a library user. Yet it seems clear that in the future it will make a great deal of sense for libraries to have materials stored in this format as well as in hard copy. In many of our interviews with academic librarians, we raised questions about the possibility of this future development. The most frequent response indicated that librarians envisioned this as an innovation of the very distant future and preferred not to explore the consequences of this technical capacity on the structure and function of academic libraries.

Bases of Authority

Individuals are capable of a wide range of behaviors; yet even the most casual observations indicate that there is remarkable uniformity in human behavior. One major line of reasoning in social-science theory posits that uniformity in behavior is caused by the exercise of various types of authority. From one perspective, the principal goal of the social sciences is precisely to understand what authority is and thus to understand more fully the dynamics of human behavior.

Max Weber exerted an extraordinary influence on the social sciences with his explication of the concept of imperative coordination, which is the tendency of members of social collectivities to obey the orders, directions, or commands issued by a legitimate source.[2] Weber distinguished among three types of legitimate authority in groups:

1. *Legal authority*—based on common acceptance of rational rules and the right of persons in authority by virtue of those rules to issue orders to others
2. *Traditional authority*—based on commitment to past values and practices and recognition of the legitimate status of those in authority by virtue of their adherence to those values
3. *Charismatic authority*—based on devout recognition of the extraordinary qualities of one particular individual and obedience to the values which she or he specifies as legitimate.[3]

Legal authority characterizes the modern bureaucracy, and this perspective typically is used in the study of complex organizations by social scientists today. Although originally analyzed in great detail by Weber, the traditional and charismatic bases of authority have been ignored for the most part by students of modern complex organizations. Our case studies of seven academic libraries make clear that they have strong components of both traditional and charismatic authority in their overall structure and function. Weber pointed out that imperatively coordinated groups very rarely belong to only one of these pure types.[4] Conformity to orders and directives and widespread uniformity of behavior in organizations draw on elements of all three bases of authority, and the study of academic libraries from an organizational perspective highlights their interdependence.

There is a large element of traditionalism in academic libraries. We cite as an example our discussion in chapter 4 of the common practice of relying on previous distributions of materials funds in determining fund allocation. Not only is this practice common, but also it is formally recognized and acknowledged. There are other practices in academic libraries which indicate substantial reliance on traditional grounds for authority. For example, many of the librarians we interviewed indicated reluctance to cancel serials subscriptions. This would annul a long-standing practice of academic librarians—the continuation of serials subscriptions. Thus significant portions of materials budgets frequently are expended to maintain complete runs of serials titles with little or no concern for their utility to support research or instructional programs.

Many special-collections departments also exhibit traditional behaviors. Once a library starts to accumulate materials for a special collection, all too frequently it is assumed that the collection should be maintained and expanded in perpetuity. Bibliographers may also expend efforts to maintain an exhaustive collection in a particular substantive area. Several of the bibliographers interviewed in the course of the research for this book indicated that it was appropriately their responsibility to maintain comprehensive collections despite the fact that the university no longer maintained any degree programs or research institutes whose faculty or students would use the materials.

In addition to an inclination to prolong long-tried practices in academic libraries, librarians also display the influence of charismatic authority. The impact of a particular library director is frequently discernible in an academic library many decades after that person departs. This influence is partially attributable to the long-range perspective which characterizes the goals of academic libraries, that is, the collection of materials for current and future instructional and research activities. The substantive interest of a particular director frequently sets in motion a chain of events which is then continued by library staff members over a long period. The impact of the interest of a strong director on the collection can often be observed by browsing through the stacks.

The dominant impact of a single individual is not characteristic of many other types of complex organizations in our society today. For example, the impact of the investment preferences of the chairperson of the board of a bank will typically disappear within one or two years after his or her departure. This is not, however, the case with academic libraries. Once collection-development activities are initiated, all too many academic librarians prefer to sustain those activities regardless of the degree of match with current or projected needs of the user community.

As Weber pointed out, charismatic authority is not stable, because it rests on a willingness to obey the directives of one individual. If the authority is to persist, it must undergo a transition to rational-legal authority or traditional authority, or a combination of both. Weber referred to this transformation as the "routinization of charisma."[5] The persistent maintenance of a collection initiated by a strong library director is an example of such routinization.

Future studies of libraries should explore further the relative salience of legal, traditional, and charismatic authority. It may well be that the emphasis on legal authority in recent organizational studies has precluded systematic investigation of the import of traditional and charismatic authority in other contemporary organizations.

Professionalism

A professional is defined by Moore as having five characteristics:

1. A full-time occupation, which is the primary source of income
2. A continuing commitment to a set of behavioral norms
3. A competence in a body of specific knowledge relevant to practice which is obtained in formal training
4. An orientation of service
5. A stature of responsible autonomy.[6]

Expertise and autonomy, the third and fifth characteristics of professionalism, particularly intrigue many social scientists, for there is an inherent conflict between these aspects of professionalism and the legal authority which characterizes the modern bureaucratic organization. A key feature of the bureaucracy is an organizational structure in which each member is responsible to and monitored by an immediate supervisor. However, when professionals are employed in bureaucracies, their expertise may readily exceed that of their immediate supervisors. This is particularly the case when diverse types of expertise are necessary for goal accomplishment. It is exceedingly difficult, if not impossible, for a bureaucratic supervisor to exercise effective control over the performance of subordinates

Organizational Theories and Social Change

when the supervisor cannot share the expertise of all who work under this direction. Yet there is growing recognition among students of social organization that these problems have been effectively solved in a wide variety of organizations that depend on high levels of specialized knowledge for goal accomplishment. The solution seems, in fact, to require a modification of the traditional bureaucratic supervisor-supervisee relationship.[7]

Our fieldwork demonstrates that academic libraries provide a fertile site for further investigating the question of the professional in an organizational setting. For example, as a result of certain aspects of technological change, the professional status of some academic librarians is becoming greatly enhanced. This is particularly true among reference librarians who provide on-line bibliographic search services to users.

Reference departments in most academic libraries traditionally have operated passively, with reference librarians awaiting the opportunity to assist users in finding relevant materials. The traditional pattern has been for the user to approach the reference desk, ask a question directly, and receive immediate guidance. The reference librarian typically has only responded to the question and rarely gotten deeply involved in the substance of the user's quest. A user might have a repeated need for reference services during the course of a research project, but typically would call on any available reference librarian for assistance. Except for a few faculty, academic library users rarely interact with the same reference librarian over time.

But these long-standing procedures change substantially with the introduction of automated bibliographic search services. These services allow a user to define a substantive problem area with a number of descriptor terms, which are then used by the reference librarian to conduct a computer search through large bibliographic information files. The computer system then prints out full references and, in many cases, abstracts of all the available material which is relevant to the problem defined by the user. These searches are increasing in many libraries, for scholars see them as an opportunity to complete rapidly very wide-ranging literature reviews. At first, the contents of the various files tended to be of interest mainly to scientists and social scientists, but data files useful to scholarly research in the humanities are now increasingly available.

In comparison with the traditional reference interaction, the user interaction with the reference librarian is very different when on-line bibliographic data searching is being done. First, it is more formal, since the user must make an appointment with the reference librarian to discuss an on-line search. Second, since the reference librarian must learn much detailed information about the user's substantive enterprise in order to select the proper terms for the search, the user has to spend more time with the librarian in describing the substantive problem area. Thus, this interaction is much more of a collegial interaction than the traditional reference librarian-user relationship used to be. Third, the reference librarian provides the user with a product that would have taken a considerable amount of time to prepare manually, a service therefore readily recognized by the scholar as immensely valuable. Finally, most academic libraries pass some part of the costs of the search on to the user. Thus, the user is paying a fee for the services.

All these characteristics—appointments, substantive involvement, collegial interactions, and fees—typically distinguish professional-client relationships. Hence, reference librarians are perceived by others, as well as by themselves, as operating in a manner consistent with high professional status. Most of the reference librarians involved in computerized bibliographic search services reported these changes. All expressed great satisfaction with both the nature of their new activities and the quality of their interactions with users. They also acknowledged an enhanced self-concept and were enthusiastic and excited about the prospects of further developing their skills in providing these services.

Organizational Boundaries

The definition of organizational boundaries is important for both theoretical and practical reasons. Yet to define boundaries is inherently a perplexing issue, for it is seldom clear precisely where they should fall. There are three perspectives commonly employed to define organizational boundaries. Physical plant provides one fairly concrete conception of boundary. One can point readily to a central or main library building and define the perimeter of various branch units. However, using physical plant for defining organizational boundaries is not always a satisfying or clear approach. For example, a university archive may occupy space within a library facility. But the archivist may report directly to the university administration, and the staff may work part-time in the special-collections department. Thus, it may be difficult to specify precisely the boundaries of either the library or the archive.

A second perspective on the definition of boundaries focuses on the membership of an organization. One can point to all the persons who are employed by the library and who fit within its organizational hierarchy, thus identifying that collectivity as the "academic library." By default, then, all other persons are nonmembers and, therefore, are to be considered as functioning outside the boundaries of the organization. However, this definition, too, is frequently obfuscated by the many joint appointments common in academia, particularly among bibliographers in large research libraries. Many employees, for example, have a portion of their salary paid by the library and the rest paid by one or more departments or research institutes. In these instances, the employee reports to two different supervisors and is simultaneously embedded in two organizational hierarchies. Thus, tracing boundaries through membership seldom provides the desired clarity.

The third and least concrete conception of organizational boundaries identifies the individuals who carry out the tasks related to the goals of the organization. This perspective makes it relatively easy to identify those who are engaged full-time in accomplishing the major functions of academic libraries. But it also includes at least a portion of the activities of a great many others who, if one uses the two previous conceptions of organizational boundaries, are outside the organization but through their activities clearly contribute to the library's goal attainment. Faculty who devote some of their time to item selection would be included within the boundaries of the academic library by this third definition. In addition, those who work for vendors and other suppliers of library materials would similarly be included.

The question is conceptually relevant for students of social organizations, for it is necessary to define and limit the objects of investigation. It is also crucial in attempting to formulate clearly and test empirically any theoretical propositions concerning complex organizations. But there is a more practical sense in which the question of organizational boundaries is pertinent. From the perspective of library administrators and managers, it is important to recognize the persons and activities that are relevant to goal accomplishment and to develop policies and strategies that ensure effective performance from all, regardless of primary organizational affiliation. Our interviews with academic-library administrators convinced us that many are not fully cognizant of the extent to which vendors and faculty are part of the library organization. Consequently, they do not try to develop more effective strategies for ensuring acceptable performance. All too many library administrators perceive that they have no authority over vendors or faculty and, therefore, cannot ensure their cooperation in collection development. The error here is assuming that since the library lacks this authority, these individuals are consequently not members of the academic-library organization.

Our case-study data interestingly show that the boundaries of academic libraries are shifting as a result of increased participation in various types of resource-sharing consortia. Traditionally, the boundaries of academic libraries remained relatively stable over time, and until recently most library administrators were free to design and implement their own operating procedures. However, as libraries increasingly participate in different resource-sharing networks (for example, shared cataloging, collection development, and on-line bibliographic data searching), their operating procedures are increasingly being determined by other organizations.

Students of social organization have recognized that many organizational boundaries do change over time, but as yet very little is known about the causes and the consequences of the shifts. Because of the mounting rate at which they participate in various resource-sharing consortia, academic libraries are now a strategic site for investigating this phenomenon.

Conflicting Goals

As indicated in our discussion in chapter 1, the governance structure of academic libraries always entails accountability to both the institution's administration and the faculty. College and university administrations must be concerned with the overall performance of the library, and decisions have to be made concerning the allocation of funds for the library vis-à-vis the many other just demands on the budget. In the past, administrators relied on a fairly small number of indicators of library performance. As mentioned, the visibility of the library is increasing, and a larger number of statistical reports and summaries on library operations are becoming available as a result of the more widespread use of automated systems.

Another important indicator for the administration is the degree of faculty satisfaction or dissatisfaction with the library's operations and collections. Regardless of whether the library director is formally responsible to only the administration or, alternately, to some type of faculty advisory or supervisory committee, the library staff are continually attempting to convince both the administration and the faculty that they are performing to maximum efficiency given scant resources. The politics of everyday life in academia requires that library managers must be responsible to both constituencies—the administration and the faculty.

However, academic-library administrators have other constituencies as well. Because of increasing degrees of professionalism, academic librarians share a feeling of accountability to fellow professional academic librarians in other institutions as well as the official standards and unofficial norms espoused by professional associations. Library managers can ill afford to be officially censored or informally panned by their fellow professionals. As participation in resource-sharing consortia increases, academic librarians find themselves responsible to another constituency—consortia members. And finally, in public academic institutions that have multiple campuses under one statewide administration, an additional constituency is emerging for academic librarians. Many multiple-campus universities are establishing universitywide library systems, and library directors find that increasingly they are accountable to both the administration on their local campus and the administration in the broader system.

Consequently, academic-library directors today have multiple constituencies to whom they are accountable for different and sometimes overlapping aspects of their operations. These different constituencies have particular interests in different aspects of the library's operations, and library managers frequently find that it is necessary to employ different means to convince different constituencies of their effectiveness.

In the literature on organizations, the concept of multiple constituencies and conflicting goals has been discussed in several studies. For example, it has been pointed out repeatedly that in medical hospitals there is a dual hierarchy which governs the organization. On the one hand, there is the medical organization consisting of doctors assigned to different departments or wards in the hospital. Those in the medical hierarchy are concerned primarily with the delivery of medical services to the patients. On the other hand, there is an administrative hierarchy which is concerned with nonmedical services, including maintenance of the facility, accounting and fiscal control, food services, and so on. There are a number of persons in the hospital, such as nursing staff, who find that they frequently are subject to control and supervision from both hierarchies, a situation which often results in conflicting expectations of performance.

Dual hierarchies such as those found in medical hospitals also now exist in academic libraries. For example, branch librarians frequently are subject to control and supervision from both the library administration and the faculty in the department which the branch serves. Other multiple hierarchies are beginning to appear. For example, the budget and planning offices of libraries in multicampus systems frequently find themselves equally responsible to the systemwide administration and the local campus administration. In addition, cataloging departments in academic libraries which rely heavily on OCLC for shared cataloging information find themselves increasingly directed by and responsive to a network administration. As the number of constituencies continues to grow for academic libraries and the control and influence which they exert over library operations expand, factions may develop within the organizational structure and create managerial problems for overall coordination and control of library activities.

Policy Implications

We have now completed the presentation of findings from the research project. Thus far, we have reviewed overall organization in academic libraries (chapter 1), the methods employed in our case studies (chapter 2), profiles of the seven institutions (chapter 3), and the details of collection development, including fund allocation (chapter 4) and item selection (chapter 5). We have demonstrated a range of variability in collection development across the seven institutions. Furthermore, we pointed out that collection development is the execution of long-range education policies, and we have expressed our concern that these policy decisions are being made without requisite knowledge or support available to academic librarians. Finally, we have raised a number of important theoretical issues in the study of complex organizations which can be fruitfully extended through the examination of academic libraries.

We now go beyond our data collection and analyses and present a set of observations relevant to future policies for collection development in academic libraries. In doing so, we are also making comments on academic librarianship more generally. We point to a number of phenomena that we perceive as barriers to change and adaptation in academic libraries. We do so not to make recommendations, but to ask questions and promote discussion.

These comments are addressed to college and university administrators, academic-library administrators, faculty and administrators in graduate schools of library and information science, and public and private funding agencies. Our analyses are not based on decades of experience as practitioners in academic librarianship. Nevertheless, they are put forth without caveat and with the intention that they will arouse interest, suggest new perspectives, and provoke fruitful deliberations of alternate solutions to a variety of problems confronting the profession of academic librarianship.

In this section we address four topics: library instruction, special collections, microforms, and research and development. Here we are attempting to be especially provocative, and in some instances we may even caricature.

Library Instruction

The first topic is library instruction, which has important long-range implications for collection development. Earlham College was particularly instructive for us with respect to this issue. Earlham has an unusually effective program for teaching library users how to identify, locate, and use materials in both their library and other institutions. As mentioned in chapter 3, the Earlham College library staff and faculty work closely in integrating use of the library into almost all facets of the instructional programs. Both students and faculty are rewarded for effective use of the library, and it is clear that the library is truly the "center of the college." This attitude is universally accepted and supported, from the president to members of the freshman class. The librarian sits on the faculty-tenure review committee, and it is quite openly acknowledged that junior faculty have difficulty in gaining tenure unless they and their students are frequent and effective users of the library.

The use of the library is thoroughly integrated into many of the courses offered at Earlham. For example, a political-science course on current policy issues in U.S. government requires that each student complete a term paper reviewing a recent piece of federal legislation. The students must use a wide variety of government documents in preparing their papers, including congressional hearings on the proposed legislation, the enabling statute, rulings issued by administrative or regulatory agencies, and federal court proceedings and rulings. By the time the students have completed this course, their sophistication in using government documents exceeds that of faculty members in most other colleges and universities. This course is organized to ensure that the students learn a great deal about recent policy issues at the federal level as well as obtain detailed, first-hand knowledge of the use of government documents for scholarly research.

This type of dual payoff in both substantive knowledge and bibliographic instruction characterizes most of the courses at Earlham. This perspective also distinguishes the Earlham approach to bibliographic instruction from that of most other academic institutions. Bibliographic instruction typically is not integrated into regular course offerings. Remedial first-year English courses may contain a brief segment on use of the library, but that is frequently the only systematic instruction received by undergraduates. Graduate students may be given some instruction in an introductory seminar or research-methods course. In very few other instances have we discovered courses at either the undergraduate or the graduate level that have formal bibliographic instruction as one of their stated goals.

Many reference librarians provide individual instruction to users while helping them solve specific reference problems. Frequently, reference librarians may be invited to give one or two lectures in a departmental course. But it is correct to characterize library staff as generally being passively responsive to requests for assistance in bibliographic instruction. Most of the faculty with whom we discussed this problem thought that it was the responsibility of the library to provide this instruction. All the library administrators would like to have greater resources to devote to library instruction, but they are unable to give such instruction a high priority. Correspondingly, college and university administrators have not viewed the problem as critical enough to warrant allocating additional resources to help librarians and faculty work more effectively in teaching students how to use the library.

Recently, Allen Kent and his colleagues published results of studies indicating that almost 40 percent of a library's collection is never used.[8] Others have estimated that 90 percent of the use of an academic library's collection involves only 10 percent of the holdings.[9] These studies have generated a great amount of controversy among academic librarians; and, with some justification, they have been criticized for methodological problems. Nevertheless, our impression, based on the seven case studies, is that very large portions of many academic-library collections are seldom, if ever, used. Many librarians are not perplexed by this fact, for in their opinion the major function of the library is to collect materials for future scholarly research.

There is a common dichotomy of values among academic librarians concerning the goals of the library. On the one hand, some see their role as facilitators of the use of current library materials; on the other, many librarians see themselves as gatherers and warehousers of materials for future scholarly research. Nevertheless, it certainly would be consistent with both these positions to increase the level of usage of the materials currently maintained by the library. Improved programs of bibliographic instruction would be of inestimable value.

To this end, vastly increased efforts should be made in bibliographic instruction for all undergraduate and graduate students. As long as bibliographic instruction is relegated to remedial or introductory courses, it will never attain the position of importance it deserves. It will, however, be exceedingly difficult to integrate bibliographic instruction in most programs of higher education, because the students' ignorance of the library is probably exceeded only by that of most faculty.

It is true that in some disciplines research and instructional activities do not depend very heavily on the library's resources. Nevertheless, if college and university administrators wish to ensure that all students are given adequate instruction as an integral part of their training, they should identify the many disciplines in which bibliographic expertise is necessary for effective professional performance. In these subject areas, there are likely to be faculty members who are interested and informed bibliophiles, and they should be supported in demanding appropriate levels of bibliographic sophistication among their students. Our few case studies have not made clear whether it would be more appropriate to assign primary responsibility for such instruction to the faculty, to the library staff, or to both. However, it is clear that higher priority should be given to this topic by all parties concerned with effective higher education.

Producing more bibliographically sophisticated users can impact future user expectations as to the appropriate scope of a library's collections. The faculty and students at Earlham, for example, conceive of their library principally as a reference library, that is, a collection of materials and services that can help them identify and locate documents needed for their scholarly work. The Earlham community does not, of course, expect that the library will contain all the materials they need for their research and instructional activities. Earlham library users anticipate that they may have to resort to other libraries. Consequently, they plan their work with sufficient lead time to allow for delivery of materials through the different lending systems in which Earlham participates.

With very few exceptions, faculty in other institutions believe it is quite appropriate to request and, in many cases, demand that their library obtain as a permanent part of the local collection all the materials they might need for both research and instructional activities. However, as we have reiterated above, academic libraries can no longer respond to all such demands. In the 1960s the materials budgets of academic libraries usually were sufficient to cover all requests for purchases. But this is certainly not the case today, and it is unlikely that it will be so in the near future. Therefore, it is necessary to produce new cohorts of academic library users who have much more realistic expectations.

It is clearly in the best interests of academic librarians to bring about this transformation of attitudes and expectations among their users. It is also in the best interests of the faculty to promote sensible expectations and to bring about more realistic perspectives concerning the amount of time required for delivery of interlibrary loans. Improved instruction can go a long way in changing the attitude of all users of academic libraries.

Special Collections

The second topic we have selected for more detailed analysis of policy implications is special collections. As described in chapter 1, special collections are a major activity of academic libraries. In both chapter 1 and chapter 3, special collections are discussed at some length. Yet in chapter 4, on fund allocation, and in chapter 5, on item selection, special collections are barely mentioned.

The absence of extended discussion of special collections in these chapters is explained by the fact that in most libraries very little, if any, of the materials budget is allocated for adding new items to the special collections. New acquisitions for these collections typically are acquired with the income of dedicated endowment funds or special funds raised for the purchase of specific materials. Therefore, it appears that special collections are not being expanded with materials funds, already in exceedingly short supply in academic libraries. However, digging further into this issue, we uncovered data sufficient to convince us of the salience of special collections for a study of collection-development policies and practices in academic libraries.

Special collections do draw substantially from the total resources available to academic libraries. Among the five university libraries studied, an average of four full-time professional library staff members are employed in special collections. Four professional librarians easily cost in excess of $80,000 per year for salaries and fringe benefits. Also, in the university libraries, between 5 and 10 percent of the floor space in the main library buildings is occupied by the special collections. The rare books and other esoteric materials included in special collections typically require special controls for temperature and humidity which are more sensitive than those used throughout the rest of the library buildings. These climate-control devices always require additional expenditures for installation, operation, and maintenance. In addition most special-collections personnel limit access to their materials and, therefore, require extra expenditures for control and security purposes. Many special-collections areas are also provided with additional security devices in the form of alarms. Finally, many special-collections departments have exceptional furnishings in reading areas. It is not possible for us to estimate total additional costs either in absolute dollars or in relative proportions of the overall library budget which are attributable to the maintenance, expansion, and utilization of special collections. But it is certainly clear that the very small proportions of the fund-allocation budgets assigned to special collections grossly underestimate the total cost to academic libraries of maintaining these materials.

In the course of our fieldwork, library administrators and special-collections librarians were asked regularly to describe how various special collections in the library had been initiated. The responses fell into two major categories. The first were narratives of how one person had donated his or her collection of rare and valuable materials. All too frequently the libraries accepted these donations without securing additional funds to provide for receiving, organizing, housing, and facilitating the use of the collection. All these additional expenses above and beyond the original donation of the materials have subsequently been borne by the library. The other major source of special collections was identified as the particular interest of faculty members. Frequently faculty members convinced the library to establish a special collection, because they had additional outside funds for obtaining rare and valuable materials. However, faculty members always retire or move to another institution. Thus they leave the library with a special collection for which there may no longer be either local demand or sources of support.

Most of the libraries we investigated maintain substantial holdings in their special collections department, but frequently they are not used by students or faculty members of the host institution. Nevertheless, special-collections librarians understandably wish to maintain and expand their collections as being valuable in and of themselves, despite the fact that there is no evidence of their present or future utility.

One special-collections librarian identified a large set of materials which represented the interests of a very distinguished faculty member who had retired over ten years ago. We asked why this special collection was still being maintained and expanded when no one had used it for a very long time and when there was no indication that utilization would increase. The librarian indicated that the collection was a great source of pride to both the library and the university. We asked this librarian why he did not pack up this collection and send it to an institution where it would be used. The question was clearly not welcomed.

In the course of the project, it also became clear that some libraries are increasing their activities in special collections for a new and most important purpose. In addition to collecting rare and valuable old books and other materials, some special-collections departments are serving as archival repositories for social and political documentation of the contemporary world. Some collect the papers of significant personalities and organizations; others collect documents on social movements and causes. Obviously, these materials will be an invaluable resource for future scholarly research, and the world will owe a debt of gratitude to those who now accumulate, index, and store these cultural records. But it seems quite legitimate to us to question seriously whether academic libraries are the appropriate locus for these costly archival activities.

Given projected fiscal constraints on academic libraries, administrators, faculty, and librarians should review jointly all activities within their special-collections departments to determine the appropriateness of using university resources (whether materials funds, salaries, or space) for the maintenance and further expansion of these materials. The primary criterion to use in making these assessments should be the degree of fit between the content of a special collection and the present and long-range educational goals of the institution. At this juncture, library directors should carefully monitor all proposals to establish new special collections, weighing the consequences of diverting resources to new collections against the additional drain on general library resources. We are, of course, not suggesting that special collections be eliminated or discontinued or that efforts be made to prohibit new special collections. Rather, one would want to prevent the establishment of haphazard or whimsical collections which no one can afford. What is needed is close review and supervision of a significant but expensive enterprise. The reviews should be both cogent and stringent.

University administrators may also wish to review carefully the opportunities for research and instructional activities afforded by existing special collections in their institutions with a view toward encouraging maximal use of these costly materials. For example, one institution we visited houses an internationally famous collection that is used heavily by visiting scholars. Yet very few of its current faculty or students use these materials. The institution is contributing scarce and needed resources to maintain and expand a collection that contributes little to its own primary goals. Thus it might be wise and prudent for university administrators to review carefully their resources and encourage faculty to mine the treasures already on their campuses.

We recognize the heresy of having university administrators recommend appointments to faculty positions in their institutions. It is possible, however, within reason, for administrators to encourage the appointment of new permanent faculty who can effectively exploit existing resources in accordance with their academic interests and pursuits. The president of a university might similarly point out the wisdom of awarding tenure to those whose scholarly interests will ensure increased use of special collections. If local treasures are not to be used locally, it places an unusually heavy burden on administrators to justify recommending investment in special collections to their boards of trustees or state legislatures. Governing boards may feel that because of present stringencies they can no longer approve using large sums of money to support special collections when they are forced to cope with numerous worthy causes, among them sorely needed increases in faculty salaries or student stipends. The maintenance of special collections which contribute to only the reputation of the institution may have become a privilege which is no longer affordable. For example, recently it has come to our attention that the board of trustees of a private institution has given serious consideration to selling a special collection to raise money to cover an immediate fiscal crisis. The proximate realities of financial considerations can easily lead to such drastic considerations and to limited perspectives inimical to the scholarly mission of universities. Some academic librarians feel uncertain about their ability to convince governing boards and state legislatures of the necessity for continued support of these activities. But any effort to conceal or disguise either the costs or the scholarly importance of special collections cannot ultimately succeed.

Microforms

As the third topic for policy consideration related to collection development, we selected microforms. The production of microforms is rapidly expanding and changing; inevitably, there is growth in both volume and format. Yet most academic libraries have not adjusted adequately to these changes. Consequently, they are not using microforms effectively to support the instructional and research programs of their host institutions. After reviewing a number of reference works describing microforms and their potential value to academic libraries, one concludes that there is an extraordinary opportunity to obtain significant portions of collections in microform, thereby saving much money and storage space and consequently easing some pressing fiscal problems.[10] Yet this potential is, for the most part, unrealized.

How widespread is the distribution of microforms in academic libraries? Unfortunately, this question is not easily answered, for librarians have not yet agreed on a uniform set of procedures for counting microform holdings. Microforms come in a wide variety of formats. The Association of Research Libraries (ARL), for example, counts microforms in four categories: reels of microfilm, number of microcards, number of microprint sheets, and number of microfiches. But not all libraries use these categories, and the information published by ARL has many gaps.[11] Regardless of the problems involved in getting accurate counts of microform holdings, the available data clearly indicate that academic libraries vary tremendously in the size of their microform collections. Among the seven institutions we studied, counts range from 24,000 to 56,000 in the two colleges and from 240,000 to 1,800,000 among the five universities. These figures make it clear that libraries are investing different proportions of their funds in microforms.

The interviews conducted during the case studies reveal that existing microforms receive minimal use. There appear to be three major reasons for the lack of use: little need for the types of material available in microform, inadequate bibliographic access, and unacceptable reading facilities. Frequently there is very little congruence between the research and instructional needs of the user community and the content of the microform collections. With the exception of certain periodicals and newspapers, most of the materials purchased by academic libraries are simply not available in microform. The suppliers of microform materials, as listed in the 1978 *Guide to Microforms in Print*, number approximately 250, but there are fewer than ten major companies in microform production.[12] The bulk of the materials listed in the *Guide to Microforms in Print* are back issues of newspapers and magazines and copies of local historical data files.

In too many cases, additions to microform collections are materials which the library would not consider purchasing in hard copy. Microforms commonly acquired by university libraries are large sets of materials organized around a general topical theme, such as major works in U.S. literature from the Colonial period to the present, or collections of important publications of U.S. government agencies. These sets frequently contain several thousand items. They may be offered for one-time purchase, or they may be offered on an annual subscription basis, with new items added each year. The collections cover many substantive areas and vary in price from several hundred to several thousand dollars.

It is frequently the case in public institutions that additional acquisitions funds become available as the end of a fiscal year approaches. However, these funds usually cannot be carried as credits into the new fiscal year and must be expended immediately. Many academic librarians are confronted with both the opportunity and the problem of spending many thousands of dollars within a very short time. Unless the library staff has maintained a substantial, current list of materials they wish to acquire, usually referred to as a desiderata list, it is virtually impossible to select enough titles to cover the funds available. Furthermore, there is a limit to how many single titles can be processed through an acquisitions department in a short time. Hence single titles that are both expensive and of reputed scholarly value become attractive end-of-year purchases. Large microform sets fit this description.

Because these sets cover broad and general topics, often it is difficult to assess quickly their potential utility in support of specific instructional or research activities. It often happens, too, that many of the individual items included in a large set are already in the collection, thus frequently resulting in substantial duplication of hard-copy materials. Consequently, many academic libraries purchase large microform sets of little value to the library's users. In one of the seven libraries studied, a large number of microform sets remained unopened in the original shipping boxes. Apparently no pressing need existed for these collections when they were ordered, and in the intervening several years since receipt no demand existed for even opening the cartons.

A second major factor in the neglect of microforms is the frequent lack of bibliographic tools to access the materials. Microform producers typically provide inadequate aids for locating materials or information within the sets. This situation not only discourages the potential user from trying to locate materials but also prevents any kind of informed or organized browsing. The problem of access to microforms is exacerbated all too frequently by the reluctance of academic librarians to catalog fully a microform collection. We have seen an instance in which a single card in the public catalog described several thousand items in a large microform collection of major literary works. Unless the user already has detailed knowledge of the contents of the microform collection, a single card in the catalog will do absolutely nothing to promote use, let alone decrease the number of requests to acquire new hard-copy materials that may be included in a microform set.

Third, with the exception of Stockton State College, none of the institutions we studied had adequate facilities for reading microforms. The reading and projection equipment was usually obsolete and typically placed in a location that does not encourage or facilitate scholarly use. We have been advised that it is a rare academic library that places its microform reading equipment in an environment convenient to the user and conducive to sustained scholarship. Typically, a microform reading room is located in a basement, an attic, or a similarly remote area.

In our view, microforms have a vastly unexploited potential for aiding academic libraries in confronting their many fiscal problems. But a variety of steps need to be taken by different agencies before this potential can be realized. First, a careful analysis should be completed of the consequences of employing different incentives for encouraging the production of microforms of more appropriate materials. This is a very complex issue that requires detailed policy-analysis research. The absence of widespread and effective use of microforms in academic libraries may be viewed as a particular case of market failure. The technology is available to produce materials in microformat at a substantial cost savings over printed formats. But most of the materials currently produced in microform are not copies of the materials which academic libraries currently purchase in printed format. Obviously, the producers do not anticipate a large enough market to risk the investment, which would be substantial. Microform versions of the materials which libraries currently purchase in hard copy would have a very high utility function for libraries. But often such versions do not exist. Even if they did, it is uncertain whether libraries would have the resources to pay their price.

The classic response to such a failure of the marketplace is to provide a subsidy to ensure that the desired object will be produced and consumed. But by no means is it clear in this case where in the system the subsidies should be applied. Should they be given to the microform producer, the library, or the consumer? It is beyond the scope of this book to attempt to resolve this question. Nevertheless, research to explore alternate subsidy procedures designed to correct this failure is urgently needed.

The analysis should include the differential utility of current and retrospective materials for instructional and research activities in different scholarly disciplines. It should examine the consequences of the pricing practices employed by some journal publishers who require subscribers to accept both hard copy and microform. It should explore the potential utility of producing microforms of current materials with computer-output microform systems coupled to computer-aided printing systems. The application of videodisk technology should also be explored.

A second policy implication concerning microforms derives from our observation of the exceptionally poor bibliographic access to large microform sets. The producers of these sets apparently have not found it profitable to provide such bibliographic aids. Improved cataloging and information-retrieval aids are required to improve the ease with which these materials may be identified, located, and projected for the user. This task should not be duplicated by each individual purchaser of the sets. There is a clear need for a centralized and coordinated effort to produce better bibliographic access to the contents of the large microform sets.

Finally, with respect to microforms, administrators in higher education and library directors should exert intense efforts to upgrade the deplorable facilities for readers of microforms. Exemplary efforts like that of the microform department in the Firestone Library at Princeton University might well serve as models for other institutions. Better reader equipment and a setting which is more conducive to scholarly work are absolute essentials, but it is also necessary to supplement an improved facility with an appropriate organizational structure. A microform department should be a separate and identifiable entity. It is also absolutely necessary that more effective activities be initiated, both to inform users of the holdings in the microform collection and to provide technical assistance in using the equipment.

In our interviews we asked many librarians and faculty members about their perceptions of resistance to microforms. The responses can be summarized in three categories. First, many users were reluctant to recognize that financial constraints will undoubtedly necessitate more widespread use of microforms in academic libraries. A second typical response was that no one is very happy with this state of affairs, but library users will simply have to accept and adjust to the reality of microforms. The third category of response noted relatively little resistance to microforms among students and junior faculty. The observation was frequently offered that young persons have been raised in a culture in which the television screen is so common that they are not upset by microform projection devices.

User resistance can be greatly diminished by introducing microform reading devices that have both better resolution (therefore causing less physical strain and discomfort for the reader) and easier portability. For over a decade now, manufacturers have promised, but failed to produce, such equipment at low cost.[13] Many librarians, however, are optimistic about the imminent delivery of such equipment.

Research and Development

The final policy consideration we draw from our research experience is that there is a serious, immediate need for more effective research-and-development activities focusing on both short- and long-range issues in library management and operations. During the course of the past two years, we have become consumers of the professional literature of librarianship, with particular emphasis on academic libraries, and regular readers of what for us were a new series of journals, among them *College and Research Libraries, Library Quarterly, The Journal of Library Automation, Library Trends, Library Journal,* and *American Libraries.* In addition, we have reviewed a number of textbooks, research monographs, and doctoral theses. Although we have not completed a thorough content analysis of this literature, we have formed an impression of its scope and quality. In comparison with the research and management literature available to other professional fields such as law, business administration, public administration, education, and social work, the research literature supporting the profession of librarianship leaves a great deal to be desired. Although there are many important exceptions, the research designs employed, the methods of data analysis, and the extraction of policy implications reveal an unfortunate lack of experience and expertise in the methods of research and policy analysis.

We divide our discussion on research and development into two parts. First, we address the need for a broader and interdisciplinary perspective in the educational and training institutions that support the profession of academic librarianship. Second, we discuss a number of policy issues pertinent to resource sharing that could be effectively informed by the results of empirical research. Faculty members with advanced training in research and policy-analysis techniques are needed in senior positions in graduate library schools. These faculty should both offer courses in research methods to library school students and conduct research in library field settings to demonstrate its utility for improving library management and overall operation. During the course of our research, we have not been able to collect information on the academic backgrounds and training of library-school faculty members. It is, however, our distinct impression, after reviewing the catalogs of many accredited library schools as well as the institutional affiliations of authors of recent library literature, that too few library schools have senior faculty members trained in fields other than librarianship.

In contrast with those of other professional schools, the faculties of library schools appear to be quite parochial in their backgrounds and research interests. It would be most beneficial to broaden the disciplinary perspectives that are currently brought to bear on research and instruction in the profession of librarianship. The cross-fertilization of many disciplinary perspectives and research methodologies has been fruitful in other fields, perhaps the best examples being those of business and public administration. Many of the leading graduate schools in these fields produce scholarly journals, the articles of which are regularly followed by practitioners, who find the research and policy implications not only stimulating but also directly applicable. The library profession would benefit immensely from a series of such scholarly journals issued by the leading library schools.

As an example of the kinds of questions that we feel could be effectively resolved with the results of interdisciplinary, empirical research, we turn to the issue of resource sharing among academic libraries. Without exception, all the librarians interviewed for this book agreed that in the future no library will be able to collect all the materials relevant for the totality of instructional and research activities occurring on a campus. There are two distinct, but related, aspects of resource sharing: shared holdings and shared acquisitions. The first involves the facilitation of interlibrary lending. This system of borrowing has been in existence for many years, but it works with varying degrees of success at different institutions as well as in different parts of the country. However, several outstanding interlibrary-loan consortia do offer rapid delivery of materials at low per-item cost within geographical areas. The MINITEX system in Minnesota and the WILS system in Wisconsin are perhaps the best examples of cost-effective and heavily used interlibrary-loan systems.

As mentioned above, academic librarians currently are engaged in heated discussions of the recently established practice of charging for interlibrary loans. The institutions that charge for this service maintain that they can no longer justify the use of their institutional resources to support the instructional and research activities of other colleges and universities. The fees are intended to cover only the costs of processing interlibrary-loan requests. Many academic librarians are, however, deeply committed to the tradition of free access to library holdings and hence are critical of charges for resource sharing. They protest that patterns of interlibrary loans are shifting dramatically, as requesters now call on institutions that do not ask for fees, the borrowers thereby placing unduly heavy demands on their local resources. They also suspect that the libraries that have instituted charges want to encourage borrowers to look elsewhere for interlibrary loans. In all institutions we studied, we encountered librarians holding strong views on both sides of this issue.

Resource sharing also involves shared acquisitions; that is, a group of libraries decides to divide collection development by specific substantive area, and each library then agrees to share the materials for which it takes responsibility. Frequently, because of geographical proximity and subject specialization, this type of shared-acquisition program can be very effective as both a cost-savings device and a collection-development procedure that ensures access to a larger amount of materials. Shortly after World War II, many university libraries joined what was known as the "Farmington plan," in which collection responsibility for various subject categories of foreign materials was assigned to different libraries throughout the nation. However, over the years the Farmington plan foundered as universities found that they were sometimes amassing materials in subject categories for which there was little local demand. Both interest and support in collecting materials for remote users were difficult to maintain, and eventually the Farmington plan collapsed. A number of institutions have discussed the possibility of reestablishing such shared-acquisitions plans on a regional basis. In fact, several institutions have begun to implement such plans.

Another important shared-acquisitions program is conducted by the Center for Research Libraries (CRL) in Chicago. With support from private foundations, CRL was founded in 1949 by ten universities. It now has over sixty members, including colleges, universities, research institutions, and private corporations. With collection-development advice from member institutions, CRL has accumulated over 3 million volumes of both current and retrospective research materials covering a wide range of substantive areas. Much of the collection is in microform. Acquisitions are either deposited by member libraries or purchased with funds derived from membership fees and grant funds. Borrowed materials may be retained until no longer needed or requested by another member. Annual membership fees are based on a sliding scale.

Many academic libraries, however, have not joined the Center for Research Libraries; indeed, of the twenty largest universities in the United States, only thirteen are members. In our interviews, we encountered much skepticism concerning the cost-effectiveness of membership, given the substantial annual fees. We also heard many anecdotes about CRL members who vastly underutilized its resources by failing to inform their users about holdings.

While conducting this project we frequently met with librarians, faculty members, and administrators who were generally supportive of the concept of resource sharing but strongly opposed to any specific proposal for enhancing either type of sharing. Frequently two viewpoints were voiced. One specified that both shared holdings and acquisitions were excellent ideas for academic libraries, but local exigencies precluded effective implementation. The second was that resource-sharing consortia should be established, holding regular meetings of library staff to discuss common problems, but meetings and discussions were all that such consortia should ever attempt. Resource sharing was something to be considered for the future, but given current and future restricted budgets, libraries simply could not run the risks of entering sharing consortia that might further drain local resources.

A number of research libraries have established very effective and promising resource-sharing arrangements. Perhaps the oldest is the agreement between the University of North Carolina and Duke University to share selected aspects of collection acquisitions and holdings. More recent, but equally promising, is the agreement between Stanford University and the University of California, Berkeley. But, to date, these successful ventures typically involve institutions of relatively comparable stature and collection size. There also have been less successful efforts, combining libraries with smaller collections into consortia where the smaller institutions constantly request materials but rarely supply materials to members that have larger and more catholic holdings. The notable exceptions here are the two statewide lending systems, MINITEX and WILS. But it should be noted that both the University of Minnesota and the University of Wisconsin have received supplemental support to expand their collections and thus meet more effectively the many requests to them for loans.

In our view, effective resource-sharing arrangements will not increase significantly in academic libraries until more information is collected concerning patterns of use of academic library materials. Also more must be learned about the limited number of shared-holdings and -acquisitions arrangements presently in operation. Without the research necessary to provide a base of knowledge for planning expanded resource-sharing activities, it is difficult to design optimal new organizational arrangements. Many academic librarians make assumptions concerning patterns of library material use. We constantly heard such statements as "Scientists rarely use books, and they are only interested in current periodicals. Humanists, on the other hand, tend to require longer materials—that is, books and lengthy periodical articles." On the basis of our interviews with faculty members in many disciplines, we strongly suspect that many of the assumptions are oversimplifications. Careful studies should be made of the types of materials used in the library, circulated on campus, and received through interlibrary loan.

One frequently encounters resistance to shared-acquisitions agreements based on the assumption that they inhibit local browsing. Yet we know very little about browsing patterns across disciplines and the relative efficiency of browsing for different types of library users. All these questions are easily amenable to empirical research. It would not be expensive to conduct such studies, and the results are essential for planning and implementing resource-sharing arrangements for the future.

It will be important to understand the characteristics of existing resource-sharing organizations such as MINITEX and WILS. In addition, the patterns of use and nonuse of such institutions as the Center for Research Libraries, University Microfilms, Inc., National Technical Information Service, The Inter-University Consortium for Political Research, and the Educational Resources Information Center (ERIC) service should also be investigated to provide insight into the incentives and barriers to participation in resource-sharing activities.

An important development, which may have a profound impact on resource sharing in academic libraries, is the increasing use of on-line bibliographic data search services. These services, provided by such vendors as the Lockheed Corporation, Systems Development Corporation, and Bibliographic Reference Service, are increasingly used in colleges and universities for literature reviews on specific, substantive topics. Many librarians interviewed for this book indicated that the users of these services usually receive extensive lists of references. Users then try to locate the materials in their own libraries. However, because the data bases of the bibliographic search services are becoming increasingly comprehensive, users are more frequently encountering citations they are unable to locate. This provokes their frustration with the library's services and intensifies demands for acquiring the materials locally or obtaining them through an interlibrary-loan system with rapid delivery. It may well happen that the use of these bibliographic search services will further increase pressures for developing new resource-sharing systems.

The proposed National Periodical Center may have a profound impact on resource sharing. In April 1977, the National Commission on Libraries and Information Science recommended the establishment of a National Periodical Center with a collection of about 55,000 periodicals for lending and photocopying. Such a facility could allow many academic libraries to cancel their subscriptions to less frequently used periodicals. The Council on Library Resources has developed a technical plan for establishing and operating such a facility.[14] One of the questions routinely asked of librarians during the case studies concerned the potential impact on periodical subscriptions if such a national lending facility came into existence. The responses varied substantially, ranging from "It would be most helpful, and we would cancel many subscriptions" to "It will have absolutely no effect here, for the faculty simply will not stand for any delay in delivery time." If academic librarians find that they can rely on the lending facility to deliver rapidly copies of materials at a relatively low cost, there may, in fact, not be as pressing a need to maintain as many current or retrospective periodicals as at present. However, on the basis of our interviews with several hundred academic librarians in seven institutions, we would venture that this outcome is by no means sure. An important component of a National Periodical Center will be the program-evaluation unit recommended by the Council on Library Resources. Data collection-and-analysis activities could produce information that might then become an integral part of the development and long-range planning for the proposed center.

This discussion of research topics relevant to resource sharing has focused only on sharing of the development and use of collections. But a most important recent activity in academic libraries involves the sharing of access to bibliographic information for the acquisition and cataloging of new materials. This sharing of bibliographic data is being made possible by such organizations as OCLC, which now accommodates over 3,000 libraries, and the recently established and now rapidly expanding Research Libraries Information Network (RLIN).

A Concluding Note

In undertaking this investigation, we recognized that our lack of prior knowledge of collection development in academic libraries could be a major problem. As outsiders to the profession of librarianship, we have not been formally trained in collection development; nor have we gained this competence through years of practice, an accomplishment that characterized so many of our interviewees. However, throughout our research we attempted to convert our naïveté into a strength: as outsiders to the profession, we sought to introduce new perspectives on collection development.

Notes

1. Alvin Toffler, *Future Shock* (New York: Bantam Books, 1970).
2. Max Weber, *The Theory of Social and Economic Organization*, translated by A.M. Henderson and Talcott Parsons (Glencoe, Ill.: Free Press, 1947), p. 324.
3. Ibid., p. 328.
4. Ibid., p. 382.
5. Ibid., pp. 363-373.
6. Wilbert E. Moore, *The Professions: Roles and Rules* (New York: Russell Sage Foundation, 1970), pp. 5-6.
7. For an excellent discussion of this problem, see Alvin W. Gouldner, *Patterns of Industrial Bureaucracy* (New York: Free Press, 1954), pp. 15-29.
8. Allen Kent, *Use of Library Materials: The University of Pittsburgh Study* (New York: Dekker, 1979).
9. Daniel Gore, "The View from the Tower of Babel," *Library Journal*, September 15, 1975, p. 1061.
10. See, for example, Albert James Diaz, ed., *Microforms in Libraries: A Reader* (Weston, Conn.: Microform Review Inc., 1975), and the journal *Microform Review*, issued since 1972.
11. Carol A. Mandel and Mary R. Johnson, *ARL Statistics 1978-79* (Washington: Association of Research Libraries, 1979).
12. John J. Walsh, ed., *Guide to Microforms in Print* (Westport, Conn.: Microform Review Inc., 1978).
13. C.M. Spaulding, "The Fifty Dollar Reading Machine . . . and Other Micromarvels," *Library Journal* 101 (October 1976):2134-2138.
14. *A National Periodicals Center: Technical Development Plan* (Washington: Council on Library Resources, 1978), p. 18.

References

Abegglin, James G. *The Japanese Factory*. Glencoe, Ill.: Free Press, 1958.

American National Standards Institute, Inc. *American National Standards for Library Statistics*. ANSI Z39.7 (R1974) New York: 1968.

Argyris, Chris. *Organization of a Bank*. New Haven: Yale University, 1954.

Arrow, Frank. *Social Choice and Individual Values*. Cowles Commission Monograph 12. New York: Wiley, 1951.

Baumol, William J., and Marcus, Matityahu. *Economics of Academic Libraries*. Washington, D.C.: American Council on Education, 1973.

Blau, Peter M. *Dynamics of Bureaucracy*. Chicago: University of Chicago Press, 1955.

Bower, Joseph L. *Managing the Resource Allocation Process: A Study of Corporate Planning and Investment*. Boston: Harvard University, 1970.

The Bowker Annual of Library and Book Trade Information. New York: Bowker, 1980.

Bunn, Oliver Charles; Siebert, W.F.; and Schueneman, Janice A. *The Past and Likely Future of Fifty-eight Research Libraries: 1951-1980: A Statistical Study of Growth and Change*. Lafayette, Ind.: Purdue University, 1966.

Caudill, William. *The Psychiatric Hospital as a Small Society*. Cambridge, Mass.: Harvard University Press, 1958.

Diaz, Albert James, ed. *Microforms in Libraries: A Reader*. Weston, Conn.: Microform Review Inc., 1975.

Dudley, Norman. "The Blanket Order." *Library Trends* 18 (1970):318-327.

Elizur, Dov. *Adapting to Innovation*. Jerusalem, Israel: Jerusalem Academic Press, 1970.

Fry, Bernard M., and White, Herbert S. "Impact of Economic Pressures on American Libraries and Their Decisions Concerning Scholarly and Research Journal Acquisitions and Retention." Final Report to the National Science Foundation. Grant no. DSI 76-23592. Bloomington, Ind.: Indiana University, 1978.

Fry, Bernard M., and White Herbert S. *Publishers and Libraries: The Study of Scholarly and Research Journals*. Lexington, Mass.: Lexington Books, D.C. Heath and Company, 1976.

Giallombardo, Rose. *Society of Women: A Study of a Women's Prison*. New York: Wiley, 1966.

Goode, William J. "The Theoretical Limits of Professionalism." In *The Semi-Professions and Their Organization: Teachers, Nurses, Social Workers*, ed. Amitai Etzioni. New York: Free Press, 1969.

Gore, Daniel, "The View from the Tower of Babel." *Library Journal*, September 1975:1061.

Gouldner, Alvin W. *Patterns of Industrial Bureaucracy*. Glencoe, Ill.: Free Press, 1954.

Ianni, Francis A.J. *A Family Business*. New York: Russell Sage Foundation, 1972.

Kaufman, Herbert. *The Forest Ranger*. Baltimore: Johns Hopkins Press, 1960

Kent, Allen. *Use of Library Materials: The University of Pittsburgh Study*. New York: Dekker, 1979.

King, D.W. *Statistical Indicators of Scientific and Technical Communication, 1960-1980*. National Science Foundation, Contract No. NSF C-878, 1976.

Lipset, Seymour M.; Trow, Martin A.; and Coleman, James S. *Union Democracy*. Glencoe, Ill.: Free Press, 1956.

Machlup, Fritz. *The Production and Distribution of Knowledge in the United States*. Princeton, N.J.: Princeton University Press, 1962.

Machlup, Fritz, and Leeson, Kenneth. *Information Through the Printed Word*. Vol. 3. New York: Praeger Publishers, 1978.

Mandel, Carol A., and Johnson, Mary R. *ARL Statistics 1978-79*. Washington, D.C.: Association of Research Libraries, 1979.

March, James G., ed. *Handbook of Organizations*. New York: Rand McNally, 1965.

McAnally, Arthur M., and Downs, Robert B. "The Changing Role of Directors of University Libraries." *College and Research Libraries*, March 1973:103-125.

Metz, Paul. "Administrative Succession in the Academic Library." *College and Research Libraries*, September 1978:358-364.

Moore, Wilbert E. *The Professions: Roles and Rules*. New York: Russell Sage Foundation, 1970.

A National Periodicals Center: Technical Development Plan. Washington, D.C.: Council on Library Resources, 1978.

Presthus, Robert. "Technological Change and Occupational Response: A Study of Librarians." Final report to Office of Education, U.S. Department of Health, Education, and Welfare. Project No. 07-1804, 1970.

Samore, Theodore. *College and University Library Statistics: Analysis of NCES Survey*. New York: Bowker, 1978.

Scholarly Communication: The Report of the National Enquiry. Baltimore: Johns Hopkins Press, 1979.

Selltiz, Claire; Wrightsman, Lawrence S.; and Cook, Stuart W. *Research Methods in Social Relations*. 3d. ed. New York: Holt, Rinehart, and Winston, 1976.

References

Selznick, Philip. *TVA and the Grass Roots*. Berkeley: University of California Press, 1949.

Sloan, Elaine F. "The Organization of Collection Development in Large University Libraries." Ph.D. diss., College of Library and Information Services, University of Maryland, 1973.

Spaulding, C.M. "The Fifty Dollar Reading Machine . . . and Other Micromarvels." *Library Journal* 101 (1976):2134-2138.

Stanton, Alfred H., and Schwartz, Morris S. *The Mental Hospital*. New York: Basic Books, 1954.

Statistical Abstract of the U.S. Washington, D.C.: U.S. Government Printing Office, 1979.

Statistical Yearbook 1976. Paris: UNESCO, 1977.

Stevens, Rolland E. "Resources in Microform for the Research Library." *Microform Review* 1 (1972):9-18.

Sykes, Gresham M. *Society of Captives: A Study of a Maximum Security Prison*. Princeton, N.J.: Princeton University Press, 1958.

Toffler, Alvin. *Future Shock*. New York: Bantam Books, 1970.

Walsh, John J. ed. *Guide to Microforms in Print*. Westport, Conn.: Microform Review Inc., 1978.

Weber, Max. *The Theory of Social and Economic Organization*. Translated by A.M. Henderson and Talcott Parsons. Glencoe, Ill.: Free Press, 1947.

Index

Academic libraries: accountability of, 9, 129-130, 142-143; acquisitions budget of, 11, 70-71, 72, 73-74, 134; budget of, as part of institutional budget, 73; change in, 134-136; and commercial vendors, 14; constituencies of, 9, 129-130, 142-143; deterioration of holdings in, 12-13; effective size of, 12; functions of, 2-5; holdings in, organization of, 118; holdings of, total, 11-12, 70; and indicators of performance, 142; and inflation, 11, 71, 76; management issues confronting, 11-14; materials acquired by, 5-8; number of, 1, 70; organization of, 8-11; and serials acquistions, 76; space problems in, 12; and user needs, 11, 12, 13, 73, 134; visibility of, 14; volumes added by, 12, 70-71
Acquisitions, 3-4, 9. *See also* Collection development
Annmary Brown Library, 42-43
Authority, 136-138; charismatic and traditional, in libraries, 137-138; types of, 136
Automated activities, 134; cataloging and acquisitions data networks, 4, 159; machine-readable books and journals, 136; on-line bibliographic search services, 139, 158; on-line catalogs, 4
Automation: and incremental change, 135; conflict between traditional librarianship and, 135; and professional status, 139-140; and shifting library boundaries, 141-142

Bibliographers: compared with branch librarians, 92, 121; faculty relationship with, 122; role in collection development, 10, 92

Bibliographic instruction. *See* Library instruction
Bower, Joseph L., 69-70, 126
Branch librarians: collection-development role of, 11, 92, 123-124; compared with bibliographers, 92, 121; and multiple hierarchies, 143
Branch libraries: collection-development decision makers in, 120; collection-development problems in, 119-120; convenience of, 119; coordination among, 120; faculty involvement in collection development for, 121; organizational location of, 9; and undergraduate library, 120. *See also* Reading rooms
Brown University, 41-43; medical program, 41-42, 104; social sciences, 86; summary statistics, 66
Brown University Library, 42-46, 103-106; acquisitions budget, 45-46; acquisitions funds by discipline, 85-86, 91; automated activities, 43-44; branches, 118-119; budget cycle 45; collection-development difficulties, 46; collection-development decision makers, 44, 103; collection size, 43; expenditures, 43, 83, 85-86; facilities, 42; faculty involvement in item selection, level of, 105; faculty liaisons, 104, 105; faculty-librarian communication, level of, 105; faculty-librarian partnership, 104; fiscal crisis, 46; fund allocation, 80, 104, 116-117; funds, sources of, 45-56, 104; government documents, 86; holdings, location of, 42, 118-119, 123, 124, 125; item selection, responsibility for, 103, 104, 116-117; item selection tools,

165

Brown University Library: *(cont.)* 105-106; organization of library, 43-45; personnel resources allocated to collection development, limitations on, 105; reference librarians and collection development, 44, 103, 104-105; serials, 83, 85, 86, 92, 104; serials and monograph expenditures, 90, 91; social sciences, support for the, 86; special collections, 42, 43, 44; summary statistics, 67; undergraduate collection, 42; vendor contracts, 86, 103-104

Case studies: comparative, 19; problems with, 19-20
Cataloging, 4, 9
Causality, 30-31
Center for Research Libraries (CRL), 156-157
Central library. *See* Main library
Change in organizations: incremental nature of, 134-135; potential and actual, 135-136; resistance to, 135
Circulation, 5, 9
Complex organizations: boundaries of, 140-141; and change, 134-135; features of, 1; and multiple hierarchies, 143
Clark Library, 61, 62
Collection development, 2-3; acquisitions department's role in, 96; and charismatic authority, 137-138; as collection management, 3; compared with acquisitions, 4; complexity of, 18; expertise needed for, 13-14, 121; historical perspective on, 70-76; indirect costs of, 92; organizational location of, 10-11; personnel costs of, 92; policies and practices of, assessment of, 128; problems confronting the management of, 128-130; statements of, 127, 129; and traditional authority, 137; and user needs, 13, 128-130. *See also* Item selection

Commercial vendors, 14, 95; contractual arrangements between libraries and, 98-99; performance of, 99, 141
Current titles, 2

Data analysis, 30

Earlham College, 34; summary statistics, 66
Earlham College Library, 34-37, 100-101; acquisitions funds by discipline, 83-84, 91; budget cycle, 36; central role in academic program, 36-37; collection-development decision makers, 100-101; collection size, 34; expenditures, 36, 83-84, 85; facilities, 34; faculty involvement in item selection, level of, 101; faculty liaisons, 100; fund allocation, 80, 100, 101, 116, 117; funds, sources of, 36, 101; holdings, location of, 34, 118, 123, 124, 125; interlibrary loan, 35, 146; item selection, responsibility for, 100, 101, 116, 117; item selection tools, 100, 101; library instruction, 36, 144-145; organization of library, 34-35; reference orientation, 35-36, 146; serials, 36, 81, 83, 100-101; serials and monograph expenditures, 90, 91; summary statistics, 67; vendor contracts, 100
End processing, 4-5
Expenditures: analysis of, 134; compared with fund allocation, 81; by discipline, 91; for library materials, 70-71, 72, 73, 74; for serials relative to monographs, 89-91; changes in, for materials, 75-76

Faculty liaisons, 97-98
Farmington plan, 156
Fieldwork activities, 23-28; flexibility in scheduling of, 23; interviews conducted during, 23-27; planning for, 23; recording and storage of data

Index

collected during, 28-29; time required for, 23
Fund allocation, 2-3, 76-78, 96, 115-118; compared with expenditures, 81; determinants of, 79; faculty involvement in, 78; fiscal constraints and, 75-76, 79-80; and item selection, 95-96; and traditional authority, 137

Interviews: data recording methods during, 27-28; flexibly structured, 26; with "outsiders," 27; rapport during, 24; representativeness of data collected during, 24. *See also* Fieldwork activities
Item selection, 3; and commercial vendors, 95; communication among those involved in, 96; current compared with retrospective, 2; expertise needed for, 13-14, 121; and faculty, 97-98; faculty involvement in, level of, 98; and fund administrators, 78, 96; and the humanities, 124-125; librarians involved in, 97; motivation for making an, 5-6; principal actors in, 95; problems resulting from faculty participation in, 98; responsibility for, 96, 115-118; tools used in, 99, 125-126; and the sciences, 123-124; and the social sciences, 125

John Carter Brown Library, 42

Kent, Allen, 145

Library instruction, 144-147; and library use, 146; and user expectations, 146-147
Library schools, 155

Main library: holdings of the, 118; decision makers for collection development, 120-121; faculty involvement in collection development for the, 121-122; user identification with the, 122
Management, library: and multiple constituencies, 142-143; and organizational boundaries, 141-142; problems of, 11-14, 76, 128-130; quality of research relevant to, 154-155
Materials, library: costs of, 11, 70-71, 72; inflation and acquisition, 70-71, 74-76; machine-readable versions of, 136; motives for acquiring, 5-6; proliferation in types of, 134; publication rate of, 11, 73; types of, 6-8; use of, 84, 86, 125, 145-146
Microforms, 7-8, 150-154; bibliographic access to, 152, 153; impediments to use of, 151-152; types of, acquired by libraries, 7-8; unrealized potential of, 150; as year-end purchases, 151-152
Minnesota Exchange (MINITEX), 58, 156, 157, 158
Moore, Wilbert E., 138

National Enquiry into Scholarly Communication (NESC), 17-18, 21
National Periodicals Center, 159

Pembroke College, 41, 42
The Pennsylvania State University, 46-48; summary statistics, 66
The Pennsylvania State University Libraries, 47-51, 106-108; acquisitions budget, 51, 86-87, 106; acquisitions funds by discipline, 86, 91; automated activities, 49, 51; bibliographers, 107; branch units, 48, 49, 119; budget cycle, 50; budget inflexibility, 51; collection-development committee, 49, 51; collection-development coordinator, 49, 107; collection-development decision makers, 106-107; collection size, 47-48; collection strengths, 47;

The Pennsylvania State University
Libraries: *(cont.)*
Commonwealth College collection development, 108; expenditures, 50-51, 86-87; facilities, 47-48; faculty involvement in collection development, level of, 107, 108; faculty liaisons, 107; fund allocation, 80, 87, 106, 116, 117-118; holdings, location of, 48, 119, 123, 124, 125; interlibrary loan, 49; item selection, responsibility for, 107, 116, 117-118, 123; item selection tools, 108; library instruction, 49-50; microforms, 47; organization of library, 48-50; personnel resources committed to collection development, 107; selection-liaison librarians, 108; serials, 47, 48-49, 51, 86, 92, 106; serials and monograph expenditures, 90, 91; serials growth, containment of, 51, 107; summary statistics, 67; vendor-selected acquisitions, review of, 108; vendor contracts, 51, 106; windfalls, 50, 86-87
Professional education, 155
Professionalism: characteristics of, 138; and legal authority, tension between, 138-139
Publication rate, 11, 73
Preservation, 3, 12-13
Public services, 9-10

Reading rooms, 122-123
Reference services, 5; collection development role of librarians in, 10-11; organizational location of, 9; and professionalism, 139-140
Reliability of data, 29-30
Research methods, 20-32; comparison of alternate, 18-19
Resource sharing, 155-159; and bibliographic search services, 158; and fees, 156; need for research on, 157-158; and shifting library boundaries, 141-142

Retrospective titles, 2; difficulty acquiring, 2, 128-129

Sample selection, 20-21; initial contacts with sites, 21-22; initial site visits, 22-23
Serials, 6-7; ambiguity in the definition of, 6-7; budget constraints and, 74-76; general fund for, 92, 117; organizational location of, 9; traditional authority and continuation of, 137
Special collections, 5, 147-150; costs of, 147-148; encouraging the use of, 149-150; initiation of, 148; need for review of, 149; organizational location of, 9; and traditional authority, 137
Stevens, Rolland E., 7
Stockton State College, 37-38; funds, sources of, 39; summary statistics, 66
Stockton State College Library, 38-41, 101-103; acquisitions funds by discipline, 84, 91; audiovisual materials, 38, 81, 103; automated activities, 38-39; budget cycle, 39-40; collection-development decision makers, 101; collection-development difficulties, 40; collection-development librarian, 39, 102-103; collection-development policy, 40, 102; collection size, 38; expenditures, 40, 83, 84-85; facilities, 38; faculty involvement in item selection, level of, 102, 103; faculty liaisons, 102; fund allocation, 80, 85, 101-102, 103, 116, 117-118; funds, sources of, 39-40; holdings, location of, 118, 123, 124, 125; interlibrary loan, 39; item selection, responsibility, division of, 101, 103, 116, 117-118; item selection tools, 103; library services, flexibility in developing, 40-41; media resources, 38; microforms, 85, 152; organization of library, 39; serials, 40, 83, 84, 85, 101; serials and monograph

Index

expenditures, 90, 91; serials growth, containment of, 40; summary statistics, 67

Technical services, 9-10

University of California, Los Angeles, 59-61; summary statistics, 66
University of California, Los Angeles, University Library, 60-65, 113-115; acquisitions budget, 64-65, 113; acquisitions funds by discipline, 89, 91; bibliographers, 63, 88-89, 113, 114, 115; branches, 60-61, 62, 113, 119; budget cycle, 63-64; collection-development decision makers, 113; collection-development officer, 63; collection size, 60-61; expenditures, 64-65, 82-83, 89; facilities, 60-61; faculty involvement in item selection, level of, 115; faculty liaisons, 114, 115; fund allocation, 80, 113, 114, 116, 117-118; funds, sources of, 64, 113; holdings, location of, 60-61, 119, 123, 124, 125; item selection, responsibility, division of, 113, 114, 116, 117-118, 123; item selection tools, 115; monograph acquisitions, support of, 89; national bibliographies, use of, 114; organization of library, 61-63; serials, 89, 92, 114, 117; serials and monograph expenditures, 90, 91; shared purchases, 65; special collections, 61; state campus libraries, coordination among, 64, 65; summary statistics, 67; undergraduate collection, 60; vendor contracts, 114
The University of North Carolina, Chapel Hill, 51-52; summary statistics, 66
The University of North Carolina, Chapel Hill, Academic Affairs Library, 52-55, 108-111; acquisitions budget, 54, 109; acquisitions funds by discipline, 87, 91; bibliographers, 54, 88-89, 109, 110; branches, 52-53, 54, 109, 110, 119; budget, 54-55; collection-development decision makers, 108-109; collection-development policy, 55; collection size, 52; collection strengths, 87; expenditures, 55, 87; facilities, 52; faculty involvement in collection development, level of, 55, 109; faculty involvement in policy formation, 53; faculty liaisons, 109; fund allocation, 55, 80, 109, 110-111, 116, 117-118; funds, sources of, 55; holdings, location of, 52-53, 119, 123, 124, 125; interlibrary loan, 54; item selection, responsibility for, 55, 109, 110, 116, 117-118, 123; item selection tools, 110; library administrative board, 53, 55, 92, 109; monograph acquisitions, support of, 87; organization of library, 53-54; resource sharing, 157; serials, 54, 87, 92, 110, 117; serials and monograph expenditures, 90, 91; special collections, 52, 109; summary statistics, 76; undegraduate collection, 52, 53, 54, 109; vendor contracts, 109, 110
University of Wisconsin, Madison, 56; summary statistics, 66
University of Wisconsin, Madison, General Library System, 56-59, 111-113; acquisitions budget, 59; acquisitions funds by discipline, 88, 91; bibliographers, 57, 59, 88, 111, 112; branches, 56, 57, 58, 111, 112, 119; branches, faculty identification with, 112; budget cycle, 58-59; collection development, decentralization of, 59; collection-development decision makers, 111; collection size, 56; collection strengths, 88; expenditures, 59, 87-88; facilities, 56-57; faculty involvement in item selection, level of, 111-112; faculty liaisons, 112; fund allocation, 59, 80, 111, 116, 117-118; holdings location of, 56-57, 119, 123, 124

125; interlibrary loan, 58; item selection, responsibility for, 112, 116, 117-118, 123; item selection tools, 112-113; organization of library, 57-58; serials, 59, 88, 92, 111; serials and monograph expenditures, 90, 91; serials growth, containment of, 111; special collections, 112; summary statistics, 67; undergraduate collection, 57; vendor contracts, 59, 111

Use of library materials, 84, 86, 125, 145-146
User needs, 13, 128-130

Weber, Max, 136-139
Webster, Duane E., 21
Wisconsin Interlibrary Loan Service (WILS), 58, 156, 157, 158
Wisconsin State Historical Society, 56-57

About the Authors

Hugh F. Cline is a sociologist trained at The University of Stockholm and Harvard University. He has taught at the University of California, Santa Barbara, and Columbia University. Prior to joining the Research Division at Educational Testing Service, Dr. Cline served as a staff member and subsequently as president of Russell Sage Foundation.

Loraine T. Sinnott has had graduate training in both mathematics and the application of technology to social settings, receiving degrees from Stanford University and the University of Southern California. Prior to joining Educational Testing Service, Dr. Sinnott was on the staff of EDUCOM, the Interuniversity Communications Council, Inc.

186420